B. Diehl

Better English Pronunciation

Better English Pronunciation

Second edition

J. D. O'Connor
Professor of Phonetics in the University of London

PUBLISHED BY THE PRESS SYNDICATE OF THE UNIVERSITY OF CAMBRIDGE
The Pitt Building, Trumpington Street, Cambridge, United Kingdom

CAMBRIDGE UNIVERSITY PRESS
The Edinburgh Building, Cambridge CB2 2RU, UK
40 West 20th Street, New York, NY 10011–4211, USA
477 Williamstown Road, Port Melbourne, VIC 3207, Australia
Ruiz de Alarcón 13, 28014 Madrid, Spain
Dock House, The Waterfront, Cape Town 8001, South Africa

http://www.cambridge.org

© Cambridge University Press 1967, 1980

This book is in copyright. Subject to statutory exception
and to the provisions of relevant collective licensing agreements,
no reproduction of any part may take place without
the written permission of Cambridge University Press.

First published 1967
Second edition 1980
Twenty-fourth printing 2002

Printed in the United Kingdom at the University Press, Cambridge

A catalogue record for this book is available from the British Library

ISBN 0 521 23152 3 Student's Book
ISBN 0 521 26349 2 Set of 2 cassettes

Contents

Acknowledgements   vii

Foreword to the second edition   ix

1 Problems in pronunciation   1
   1.1   Introduction   1
   1.2   'Lend me your ears'   3
   1.3   Which English?   5
   1.4   The basic sounds   6
   1.5   Letters and sounds   7
   1.6   Sounds and sound-groups   9
   1.7   Words and utterances   11
   1.8   Exercises   12

2 How the speech organs work in English   13
   2.1   The vocal cords   13
   2.2   The palate   15
   2.3   The teeth   17
   2.4   The tongue   17
   2.5   The lips   21
   2.6   Exercises   22

3 The consonants of English   24
   3.1   Friction consonants: /f, v, θ, ð, s, z, ʃ, ʒ, h/   24
   3.2   Stop consonants: /p, b, t, d, k, g, tʃ, dʒ/   39
   3.3   Nasal consonants: /m, n, ŋ/   48
   3.4   Lateral consonant: /l/   53
   3.5   Gliding consonants: /j, w, r'/   57
   3.6   Exercises   63

4 Consonant sequences   64
   4.1   Initial sequences   64
   4.2   Final sequences   67

Contents

- 4.3 Longer consonant sequences 76
- 4.4 Exercises 78

5 The vowels of English 79
- 5.1 Simple vowels /iː, ɪ, e, æ, ʌ, ɑː, ɒ, ɔː, ʊ, uː, ɜː, ə/ 79
- 5.2 Diphthongs /əʊ, aʊ, eɪ, aɪ, ɔɪ, ɪə, eə, ʊə/ 84
- 5.3 Vowel sequences 87
- 5.4 Exercises 88

6 Words in company 90
- 6.1 Word groups and stress 90
- 6.2 Stressed and unstressed syllables 91
- 6.3 Weak forms of words 92
- 6.4 The use of strong forms 95
- 6.5 Rhythm units 95
- 6.6 Fluency 100
- 6.7 Changing word shapes 102
- 6.8 Exercises 105

7 Intonation 108
- 7.1 Tune shapes 109
- 7.2 The falling tune – the Glide-Down 111
- 7.3 The first rising tune – the Glide-Up 114
- 7.4 The second rising tune – the Take-Off 116
- 7.5 The falling-rising tune – the Dive 117
- 7.6 How to use the tunes 120
- 7.7 Exercises 125

Conversational passages for practice 128

Answers to exercises 134

Appendix 1 The difficulties of English pronunciation for speakers of Arabic, Cantonese, French, German, Hindi and Spanish 138

Appendix 2 Useful materials for further study 147

Glossary 149

Acknowledgements

Every writer of a textbook owes a debt to his predecessors, to his teachers, to his colleagues and to his pupils; I gratefully acknowledge my deep indebtedness to all of these. In addition I wish to express particular thanks to Mrs M. Chan of Hong Kong, Miss Afaf M. E. Elmenoufi of Cairo and Dr R. K. Bansal of Hyderabad for very kindly helping me with regard to the pronunciation difficulties of Cantonese, Arabic and Hindi speakers respectively. Last, but far from least, my very sincere thanks go to my friends Pauline Speller, who typed the whole of a by no means easy manuscript and did it admirably, and Dennis Speller, who drew for me the original illustrations.

The responsibility for the book is mine; any credit I happily share with all those mentioned above.

J. D. O'C.

Foreword to the second edition

Since this book was first published, in 1967, my attention has been drawn by users of it to various errors and omissions, and suggestions have been made for improving its usefulness. In this second edition I have now remedied the errors and omissions and I have adopted those suggestions which I think improve the book. To all those readers who were kind enough to write to me on these matters I offer my sincere thanks.

My old readers will no doubt consider the greatest change in this edition to be the use of a different phonetic transcription, and I agree. The reason why I decided to change the transcription is this: when the book was first published I used the transcription of Daniel Jones's *English Pronouncing Dictionary* (Dent), which I considered to be the best guide to English pronunciation for foreign learners (as I still do). The present editor of the dictionary, A. C. Gimson, decided, rightly in my opinion, to change his transcription for the 14th edition of 1977. This meant that my transcription no longer corresponded to any of those found in the major dictionaries commonly used by foreign learners. I have now rectified this quite unacceptable situation by adopting the Gimson transcription which is also used in the *Longman Dictionary of Contemporary English* (1978) and the *Oxford Advanced Learner's Dictionary of Current English* (4th edition 1980).

There have often been understandable complaints from students that different writers on English pronunciation used different transcriptions. It seems to me that there is at least a movement towards using a standard transcription, namely, the one now used in this book, and this is a wholly welcome development.

The new transcription differs from the old only in the matter of symbols for the English vowels, and for the convenience of old readers I list both old and new forms below:

Old form	*Key word*	*New form*
iː	feel	iː
i	fill	ɪ
e	fell	e

Foreword

ɔː	f*a*ll	ɔː
u	f*u*ll	ʊ
uː	f*oo*l	uː
ei	f*ai*l	eɪ
ou	f*oa*l	əʊ
ai	f*i*le	aɪ
au	f*ou*l	aʊ
ɔi	f*oi*l	ɔɪ
æ	c*a*t	æ
ɔ	c*o*t	ɒ
ʌ	c*u*t	ʌ
əː	c*ur*t	ɜː
ɑː	c*ar*t	ɑː
iə	t*ier*	ɪə
ɛə	t*ear*	eə
uə	t*our*	ʊə
ə	b*a*n*a*n*a*	ə

Vowels which were previously differentiated only by the length mark (ː) are now distinguished both by the length mark and by letter-shape, e.g. fiːl/fɪl. This makes for easier visual recognition and underlines the fact that the pairs of vowels differ not only in length but also in quality.

A recording of all the practice material is available on cassettes. The symbol ▭ in the text indicates exactly what is recorded.

The book has been entirely re-designed and re-set, and the diagrams have been re-drawn; for this and much other help my thanks are due to the Cambridge University Press.

I hope that my book will continue to serve a useful purpose for both teachers and learners of English in helping them towards a better English pronunciation.

1 Problems in pronunciation

1.1 Introduction

The purpose of this book is very simple: to help you, the reader, to pronounce English better than you do now. Millions of foreign students want to learn English as well as they can; for some it is only a matter of reading and writing it, and they will find no help here. But many students want to be able to speak English well, with a pronunciation which can be easily understood both by their fellow-students and by English people, and it is for them that this book is specially intended.

Written English and spoken English are obviously very different things. Writing consists of marks on paper which make no noise and are taken in by the eye, whilst speaking is organized sound, taken in by the ear. How can a book, which is nothing but marks on paper, help anyone to make their English *sound* better? The answer to this is that it can't, not by itself. But if you will co-operate, and listen to English as much as you can, along the lines that I shall suggest to you, then you will find that the instructions given in the following pages will make your ears sharper for the sound of English and when you can *hear* English properly you can go on and improve your performance.

Language starts with the ear. When a baby starts to talk he does it by hearing the sounds his mother makes and imitating them. If a baby is born deaf he cannot hear these sounds and therefore cannot imitate them and will not speak. But normal babies can hear and can imitate; they are wonderful imitators, and this gift of imitation, which gives us the gift of speech, lasts for a number of years. It is well known that a child of ten years old or less can learn *any* language perfectly, if it is brought up surrounded by that language, no matter where it was born or who its parents were. But after this age the ability to imitate perfectly becomes less, and we all know only too well that adults have great difficulty in mastering the pronunciation (as well as other parts) of foreign languages. Some people are more talented than others; they find pronouncing other languages less difficult, but they never find them easy. Why is this? Why should this gift that we all have as

Problems in pronunciation

children disappear in later life? Why can't grown-up people pick up the characteristic sound of a foreign language as a child can?

The answer to this is that our native language won't let us. By the time we are grown up the habits of our own language are so strong that they are very difficult to break. In our own language we have a fairly small number of sound-units which we put together in many different combinations to form the words and sentences we use every day. And as we get older we are dominated by this small number of units. It is as if we had in our heads a certain fixed number of boxes for sounds; when we listen to our own language we hear the sounds and we put each into the right box, and when we speak we go to the boxes and take out the sounds we want in the order we want them. And as we do this over the years the boxes get stronger and stronger until everything we hear, whether it is our own language or another, has to be put into one of these boxes, and everything we say comes out of one of them. But every language has a different number of boxes, and the boxes are arranged differently. For example, three of our English boxes contain the sounds at the beginning of the words *fin*, *thin* and *sin*, that is, *f*, *th* (this is one sound, of course) and *s*. Like this:

f	th	s

Now, many other languages have boxes which are similar to the English ones for *f* and *s*, but they do not have a special box for the *th*-sound. And we can picture this in the following way:

f	th	s
f		s

When the foreign listener hears the English *th*-sound he has to put it in one of his own boxes, his habits force him to do so, and he has no special *th* box, so he puts it into either the *f* box or the *s* box:

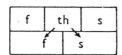

In other words, he 'hears' the *th*-sound as either *f* or *s*; a funny *f* or a funny *s*, no doubt, but he has nowhere else to put it. And in speaking the same thing happens: if he has to say *thin*, he has no *th* box to go to so he goes to the nearest box available to him, either the *f* or the *s*, and

Introduction

he says either *fin* or *sin* (or it may be *tin*, if he has a *t* box in his language).

The main problem of English pronunciation is to build a new set of boxes corresponding to the sounds of English, and to break down the arrangement of boxes which the habits of our native language have so strongly built up. We do this by establishing new ways of hearing, new ways of using our speech organs, new speech habits.

This may sound easy, but it isn't. Unfortunately, it is never easy to establish good habits, it is always the bad ones which come most naturally, and you will need to do a great deal of hard work if you want to build yourself a set of English boxes which are nearly as firm as those of your own language. Anyone who says that you can get a good English pronunciation without hard work is talking rubbish, unless you happen to be one of the very small number of lucky people to whom pronunciation comes fairly easily. Most of us need to work hard at it, and this book is for people who are prepared to work hard. If you work hard and regularly along the lines suggested in this book, you will improve. One of the most important things to remember is that *everyone can improve*, even if they have no great talent for language. Quite apart from anything else, there is great satisfaction to be got from the development of what talent you have. You may never sound like a native English speaker, but at least you will have got as close to it as you can.

1.2 'Lend me your ears'

If speech depends on hearing, and books don't talk, what are you to do? Fortunately there is a lot of English spoken about the world. On films, on the radio, on tapes, on gramophone records; most people can get the opportunity of listening to English in some way, and this is what you must do. *You must hear English.* But just hearing it is not enough; you must listen to it, and you must listen to it not for the meaning but for the sound of it. Obviously when you are listening to a radio programme you will be trying to understand it, trying to get the meaning from it; but you must try also for at least a short part of the time to forget about what the words mean and to listen to them simply as sounds. Take one of the English sounds at a time, it might be the English *t*, and listen for it each time it comes; concentrate on catching it, on picking it out, on hearing what it sounds like. Don't just be satisfied to hear it vaguely, as if it were a sound of your own language; try and pick out the Englishness of it, what makes it different from the nearest sound in your language. And when you think you have got it, then say it in some of the words that you have heard, and say it *aloud*. It is no use practising silently; all of us are much better at pronouncing if we do it silently, inside ourselves. But you can't talk English inside yourself, it has to come out, so practise aloud, even if it puzzles your family or your friends. Later in the book you will find pronunciation exercises to be done; these too must be done aloud.

Films or radio programmes have the disadvantage that you can't stop them and ask for something to be repeated. Gramophone records and tapes do not have this disadvantage. With them you can repeat any part of the text as often as you need, and you must do this: it is much better for your ear if you listen to the same passage six times than if you listen to six different passages; but be careful – listen closely each time, don't relax after two or three hearings, try to keep your ears as closely concentrated on the sound of the passage at the sixth hearing as at the first. In this way you will build up a store of sound-memory which will form a firm base for your performance.

Now, performance. When you practise (aloud, of course), you must listen carefully and accurately. If you have listened properly in the first place you will know what the English words and sentences sound like, and you must compare as closely as you can the sounds that come out of your mouth with the sounds that you are holding in your head, in your sound-memory. Don't be satisfied too easily, try to match your sounds exactly with the sounds that you have listened to.

Some of you may be able to make use of a tape-recorder; if you can, you will be able to hear what you sound like to other people and this is very helpful. If you can, record on the tape-recorder a sentence or a longer passage with which you are familiar through hearing it said by an English speaker. Then listen to it, closely and carefully, and see where your performance does not match the original; mark the places where you are dissatisfied, and practise these bits until you think you have them right; then record the passage, listen critically again, and repeat the sequence. One word of warning – a tape-recorder will not do the job for you; it is a useful instrument, but it is not a magic wand which will make your English perfect without any effort from you. It is useful only because it enables you to listen to yourself from the outside, which makes it easier for you to hear what is wrong, but it is you who have to put it right, and the machine cannot do this for you. In the end it is absolutely essential for you to be able to match what you say with your sound-memory of English. So although a tape-recorder is helpful, this does not mean that if you haven't got one your English will not improve, and, just as important, it does not mean that if you have a tape-recorder your English will necessarily be better. Careful listening is the most important thing; and careful matching of performance with listening will bring you nearer to the ideal of a perfect English pronunciation. And make no mistake, your aim must be to acquire a perfect English pronunciation. You will almost certainly not succeed in this aim because it requires, as I have said, a very rare gift; but unless this is your aim you will not make all the progress of which you are capable; keep working towards perfection until you are quite sure that it is neither necessary nor profitable for you to continue. Then you will have done yourself justice.

1.3 Which English?

What do we mean by a perfect English pronunciation? In one sense there are as many different kinds of English as there are speakers of it; no two people speak exactly alike – we can always hear differences between them – and the pronunciation of English varies a great deal in different geographical areas. How do we decide what sort of English to use as a model? This is not a question which can be decided in the same way for all foreign learners of English. If you live in a part of the world like India or West Africa, where there is a tradition of speaking English for general communication purposes, you should aim to acquire a good variety of the pronunciation of this area; such varieties of Indian English or African English and the like are to be respected and used as a model by all those who will need their English mainly for the purpose of communication with their fellows in these areas. It would be a mistake in these circumstances to use as a model B.B.C. English or anything of the sort.

On the other hand, if you live in an area where there is no traditional use of English and no body of people who speak it for general communication purposes, then you must take as your model some form of native English pronunciation, and which form you choose does not very much matter. The most sensible thing to do is to take as your model the sort of English which you can hear most often. If you have gramophone records of English speech based on, let us say, an American pronunciation, make American your model; if you can listen regularly to the B.B.C., use that kind of English. But whatever you choose to do, remember this: all these different accents of English have a great deal in common, they have far more similarities than differences, so don't worry too much what sort of English you are listening to provided it *is* English.

Problems in pronunciation

In this book I cannot describe all the possible pronunciations of English that might be useful to you so I shall concentrate on one, the sort of English used by educated native speakers in south-east England, often referred to as Received Pronunciation (R.P. for short), that is 'accepted' pronunciation. R.P. will be the basis; but I am less interested in making you speak with this particular accent of English than in helping you to make the necessary differences between the basic sounds which are found in all kinds of English: these are found in R.P. and because of this it is as useful to describe R.P. as to describe any other native pronunciation, and if you really want to speak with a British accent, then this is as good as any, in the sense that it is widely acceptable.

1.4 The basic sounds

The sounds at the beginning of each of the words in the following list are all different: the letters which stand for these sounds (usually one letter per sound, but sometimes two) are printed in italic type:

*p*ier	*v*eer	*n*ear
*b*eer	*sh*eer	*w*eir
*t*ier	*h*ear	*y*ear
*d*eer	*l*eer	*ch*eer
*g*ear	*r*ear	*j*eer
*f*ear	*m*ere	

It is the sound at the beginning of the word, the initial sound, which makes one word different from all the other words in the list. Since this is so, since these sounds are *distinctive*, it is obviously necessary to be able to make them sound different: they are basic sounds of English – all kinds of English. So are the sounds of the letters in italic type in these lists:

ba*se*	wra*th*
bai*z*e	wro*ng*
ba*the*	
bei*ge*	
ba*ke*	

In these lists the sounds at the end of the word are distinctive, the final sounds. If you count up the sounds which are distinctive in initial

The basic sounds

position and those which are distinctive in final position you will find that there are twenty-four altogether. These twenty-four sounds which occur initially and finally, though they occur in other positions too, are called *consonants*.

Now look at these lists:

f*ee*l	c*a*t	t*ie*r
f*i*ll	c*o*t	t*ea*r
f*e*ll	c*u*t	t*ou*r
f*a*ll	c*ur*t	
f*u*ll	c*ar*t	
f*oo*l		
f*ai*l		
f*oa*l		
f*i*le		
f*ou*l		
f*oi*l		

Most of these sounds, represented again by letters in italic type, occur surrounded by consonants, and this is typical, although most of them can also occur initially and finally too. These sounds are called *vowels*.

NOTICE

1 Five of these words, *curt, cart, tier, tear, tour*, have a letter *r* in them. In many English accents, e.g. American, Canadian, Scottish, Irish, this would be pronounced exactly like the consonant at the beginning of *red*, but in R.P. and various other accents the letter represents part of a basic vowel unit. There is more detail about this on p. 61.
2 There is one other vowel, making twenty in all, which occurs in the word b*a*nana. This is a very special and very important vowel in English and it is discussed in full on pp. 82–4.

1.5 Letters and sounds

These must never be mixed up. Letters are written, sounds are spoken. It is very useful to have written letters to remind us of corresponding sounds, but this is all they do; they cannot make us pronounce sounds which we do not already know; they simply remind us. In ordinary English spelling it is not always easy to know what sounds the letters stand for; for example, in the words c*i*ty, b*u*sy, w*o*men, pr*e*tty, vill*a*ge, the letters *i, y, u, o, e* and *a* all stand for the *same* vowel sound, the one which occurs in *sit*. And in b*a*nana, b*a*ther, m*a*n, m*a*ny the letter *a* stands

Problems in pronunciation

for five different vowel sounds. In a book which is dealing with pronunciation this is inconvenient; it would be much more useful if the reader could always be certain that one letter represented one and only one sound, that when he saw a letter he would know at once how to pronounce it (or at least what to aim at!). That is why it is helpful to use letters in a consistent way when dealing with English. We have twenty-four consonants and twenty vowels to consider and we give to each of these forty-four units a letter (or sometimes two letters, if this is convenient). In that way we can show without any doubt what the student should be trying to say.

Here again are the words listed on pp. 6–7 and this time beside each word is the letter of the International Phonetic Alphabet which will *always* be used to represent the sound to which that word is the key, however it may be spelt in other words. Most of the letters will be perfectly familiar to you, others will seem strange for a little while; but not for long.

pier /p/	fear /f/	rear /r/	cheer /tʃ/
beer /b/	veer /v/	mere /m/	jeer /dʒ/
tier /t/	sheer /ʃ/	near /n/	
deer /d/	hear /h/	weir /w/	
gear /g/	leer /l/	year /j/	
base /s/	wrath /θ/		
baize /z/	wrong /ŋ/		
bathe /ð/			
beige /ʒ/			
bake /k/			
feel /iː/	fail /eɪ/	cat /æ/	tier /ɪə/
fill /ɪ/	foal /əʊ/	cot /ɒ/	tear /eə/
fell /e/	file /aɪ/	cut /ʌ/	tour /ʊə/
fall /ɔː/	foul /aʊ/	curt /ɜː/	
full /ʊ/	foil /ɔɪ/	cart /ɑː/	banana /ə/
fool /uː/			

The use of the colon (ː) with the vowels /iː, ɔː, uː, ɑː, ɜː/ is to show that they are in general *longer* than /ɪ, ʊ/ etc. They are also different in their actual sound, as the different letters indicate.

Here are some examples of words written in this way: *city* sɪtɪ, *busy* bɪzɪ, *women* wɪmɪn, *banana* bənɑːnə, *bather* beɪðə, *man* mæn, *many* menɪ, *wrong* rɒŋ, *change* tʃeɪndʒ, *house* haʊs, *thought* θɔːt, *could* kʊd, *cough* kɒf, *rough* rʌf, *though* ðəʊ.

Letters and sounds

This way of writing or transcribing makes it possible to show that some words which are ordinarily spelt in the same way sound different; for example, *lead*, which is pronounced liːd in a phrase like *lead the way*, but led in *lead pipe*. It also makes clear that some words which are spelt differently sound the same, for example, *rain, rein, reign*, which are all pronounced reɪn.

1.6 Sounds and sound-groups

A sound is made by definite movements of the organs of speech, and if those movements are exactly repeated the result will always be the same sound; it is easy to show that there are more than forty-four sounds in English – even in the pronunciation of a single person, without worrying about differences between people. For instance, if you say *tea* and *two* tiː, tuː you will notice that the lips are in a rather flat shape for tiː but are made rounder for tuː, and this is true for both the consonant /t/ and for the two vowels. So the organs of speech are not making *exactly* the same movements for the /t/ of *tea* and the /t/ of *two*, and therefore the resulting sounds are not exactly the same. You can prove this to yourself by only saying the consonant sounds of these words: think of the word *tea* and pronounce the beginning of it – but not the vowel. Then do the same for *two*; think of the word but stop before the vowel: you can hear and feel that the two sounds are different. Obviously most of the movements we make when pronouncing these two sounds are the same, and they therefore sound alike, but not identical.

Take another example, /h/. When we pronounce the words *he, hat, who* hiː, hæt, huː, the /h/-sounds are different: in pronouncing /h/ we put our mouth into the position needed for the following vowel and then push out air through this position, but since the three different vowels have three different mouth-positions it follows that the three /h/-sounds must also be different. You can prove this again, as with the /t/-sounds, by saying the beginnings of these words whilst only thinking the rest.

Each of the letters we use to show pronunciation may stand for more than one sound; but each of the sounds represented by one letter has a great deal of similarity to the other sounds represented by the same letter; they have more similarities than differences: none of the /h/-sounds could be mistaken for an /l/- or an /s/-sound, and none of the /t/-sounds can be confused with a /p/- or a /k/-sound.

These groups of sounds, each represented by one letter of the phonetic alphabet, are called *phonemes*, and the method of representing each phoneme by one symbol is called *phonemic transcription*. Phonemic transcription may be enclosed in diagonal lines /........./. It is necessary to distinguish carefully between phonemes and sounds: the 44 phonemes of English are the basic contrasts which make it possible for us to keep each word or longer utterance separate from every other, fiːl from fɪl and pɪə from bɪə, etc. But each phoneme may be represented by different sounds in different positions, so the different /t/-sounds in *tea* and *two* both represent the /t/ phoneme, and the three /h/-sounds in *he, hat, who* all represent the single /h/ phoneme.

This suggests two stages in the learning of pronunciation: the first is to be able to produce 44 vowels and consonants which are different, so that the words and longer utterances of English do not at any rate sound the same, so that fiːl and fɪl sound different. At this stage the learner will not worry about which of the possible /h/-sounds he is using; any of them will serve to distinguish *heat* hiːt from *eat* iːt. If the common feature of each phoneme is reproduced, all the necessary distinctions of words, etc., can be made. But obviously if the learner uses a particular sound in a word where an English speaker uses a different sound belonging to the same phoneme, the effect will be odd; he will not be misunderstood – that could only happen if he used a sound belonging to a different phoneme – but he will not be performing in an English way, and if this happens with many of the phonemes it will contribute to a foreign accent. So the second stage in learning pronunciation must be to learn to use as many different sounds as is necessary to represent a particular phoneme. In theory a single phoneme is represented by a different sound in every different position in which it occurs, but most of these differences will be made automatically by the learner without instruction. It is only in cases where this is unlikely to happen that it will be necessary to worry about particular sounds within a phoneme.

There is one other relation between sound and phoneme which is likely to give trouble. Here is an example: in English /d/ and /ð/ are different phonemes; in Spanish there are sounds which are similar to those used in English to represent these phonemes – we can write them /d/ and /ð/; but in Spanish these two sounds belong to the *same* phoneme – when the phoneme occurs between vowels it is represented by /ð/, as in *nada* 'nothing', but when it occurs in initial position it is represented by /d/, as in *dos* 'two'. This will cause difficulty for the Spanish speaker because although he has more or less the same sounds as in English he is not able to use them independently, and whenever

Sounds and sound-groups

an English /d/ occurs between vowels he will be in danger of using /ð/, and confusing *breeding* briːdɪŋ with *breathing* briːðɪŋ, and whenever English /ð/ occurs in initial position he will be in danger of using /d/, confusing *they* ðeɪ and *day* deɪ. In general, if two sounds belong to one phoneme in your language, but to two different phonemes in English there will be danger of confusions until you have learnt to forget the habits of your language and use the sounds independently as in English. This can be done by careful listening and accurate use of the speech organs and a great deal of practice.

1.7 Words and utterances

Most of what I have said so far has been about the pronunciation of short pieces of speech, sounds or single words; it is necessary at first to be sure that the basic sounds of the language are being properly pronounced and the best way of doing that is to practise single words or very short phrases; but we do not talk in single words, and certainly not in single sounds. The sounds and words are connected together with others to make up longer utterances, and these longer utterances have special difficulties of their own.

First, they must be pronounced smoothly, without hesitations and without stumbling over the combinations of sounds. It may be quite easy to pronounce separately the words, *library, been, lately, you, to, the, have*, but it is much more difficult to pronounce the question *Have you been to the library lately?* without hesitating and without making mistakes.

Secondly, in a longer English utterance some of the words are treated as being more important to the meaning than others, and it is necessary to know which these words are and how they are treated in speech. And words which are not regarded as being particularly important often have a different pronunciation because of this; for example, the word *can* which is pronounced kæn if it is said by itself, is often pronounced kən in phrases like *You can have it* juː kən hæv ɪt.

Thirdly, the rhythm of English must be mastered. That is, the different lengths which the syllables of English are given and the reasons why these different lengths occur. An example of this would be the following:

The c h a i r collapsed.
The chairman collapsed.

The word *chair* has the same length as the word *chairman*, and therefore

Problems in pronunciation

each of the two syllables in *chairman* is shorter than the single syllable of *chair*, so that the *chair* of *chairman* is only half as long as the word *chair* by itself.

Fourthly, and last, the tune of the voice, the melody of speech is different in different languages and it is necessary to learn something of the English way of using tune. For example, when we say *thank you*, the voice may go from a higher note to a lower one, or it may go from a lower note to a higher one and these two different tunes show two different attitudes: higher to lower means sincere gratitude; lower to higher means that the matter is purely routine. To confuse the two would clearly be dangerous and it is necessary to learn what tunes there are in English and what they mean.

All these matters will be dealt with in the chapters which follow, and exercises will be given to help the reader to improve his performance at each stage. But the first important thing is to be sure that the basic sound-distinctions are right and this requires knowledge of the working of the speech organs; this is the subject of the second chapter.

1.8 Exercises

(Answers on p. 134)

1. How many *phonemes* are there in the following words (the lists on p. 8 will help you here): *write, through, measure, six, half, where, one, first, voice, castle, scissors, should, judge, father, lamb*?
2. *Bear* and *bare* are spelt differently but pronounced the same, beə. Make a list of other words which are spelt differently but pronounced in the same way.
3. Write the words in Exercise 1 above in *phonemic* transcription, and then memorize the forty-four symbols needed to transcribe English phonemically so that you can do it without looking at the lists. Now transcribe the following words phonemically: *mat, met, meet, mate, might, cot, cut, caught, lick, look, bird, board, load, loud, boys, bars, bears, sheer, sure, copper, green, charge, song, five, with, truth, yellow, pleasure, hallo*.
4. Try to make lists like those on p. 8 for your language, and see how many phonemes it uses. For some languages this will be quite easy, for some it will be difficult; if you have difficulty in finding words which are different only in one phoneme, find words which are as similar as you can. An English example of this kind is *getting, cutting* (which shows that /g, k/ and /e, ʌ/ are different phonemes). What phonemes does the pair *mother, father* separate?

2 How the speech organs work in English

In all languages we speak with air from the lungs. We draw it into the lungs quickly and we release it slowly and then interfere with its passage in various ways and at various places. Figure 1 is a diagram showing a side view of the parts of the throat and mouth and nose which are important to recognize for English.

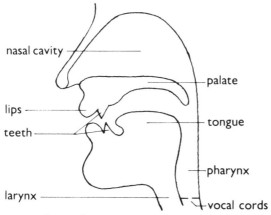

Fig. 1 *The speech organs*

2.1 The vocal cords

The air released by the lungs comes up through the wind-pipe and arrives first at *the larynx*. The larynx contains two small bands of elastic tissue, which can be thought of as two flat strips of rubber, lying opposite each other across the air passage. These are the vocal cords.

The inner edges of the vocal cords can be moved towards each other so that they meet and completely cover the top of the wind-pipe, or they can be drawn apart so that there is a gap between them (known as *the glottis*) through which the air can pass freely: this is their usual position when we breathe quietly in and out.

When the vocal cords are brought together tightly no air can pass

The speech organs

through them and if the lungs are pushing air from below this air is compressed. If the vocal cords are then opened suddenly the compressed air bursts out with a sort of coughing noise. Try this: open your mouth wide, hold your breath, imagine that you are picking up a heavy weight, holding it for two seconds, then dropping it and suddenly let your breath out. This holding back of the compressed air followed by a sudden release is called *the glottal stop*, and what you feel as the air bursts out is the vocal cords springing apart. Do this ten times, and get used to the feeling of the 'click' of the vocal cords as they release the air. The compression of the air may be very great, as when we do lift a heavy weight, or it may be quite slight, when the result is like a very gentle cough.

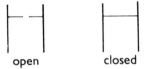

Fig. 2 The vocal cords

If the vocal cords are brought together quite gently, the air from the lungs will be able to force them apart for a moment, but then they will return to the closed position; then the air will force them apart again, and they will close again, and so on. This is a very rapid process and may take place as many as 800 times per second. It is obviously not possible to hear each individual 'click' of the opening vocal cords, and what we do hear is a musical note. The height of the note depends on the speed of opening and closing of the vocal cords; if they open and close very quickly the note will be high, if they open and close slowly the note will be low. The note, whether high or low, produced by this rapid opening and closing of the vocal cords is called *voice*.

Some of the English sounds have voice and some do not. Say a long /m/-sound and put your fingers on your neck by the side of the larynx. You will feel the vibration of the vocal cords. Now keep your lips closed still, but just breathe hard through your nose: no vibration. Repeat this several times, first /m/ then breathe through the nose, and get used to the feeling of voice and no voice. Now say the word *more* mɔː, still with your fingers on your neck. Does the vowel /ɔː/ have voice? Can you still feel the same vibration for /ɔː/ as for /m/? Yes, both sounds are voiced. Say a long /s/-sound. Is it voiced? No, it has no vibrations. Try other sounds of your own language and English and see which of them are voiced and which not.

The vocal cords

The sounds which are not voiced – *voiceless* sounds – are made with the vocal cords drawn apart so that the air can pass out freely between them and there is no vibration. The difference between voiced and voiceless can be used to distinguish between what are otherwise similar sounds. Say a long /s/-sound again, and in the middle of it turn the voice on: this will give you a /z/-sound, buzzing rather than hissing. But not all the voiced sounds of English have similar voiceless sounds, for example the voiceless /m/-sound which you made just now does not occur in English, and even when there are pairs of similar sounds which are voiced and voiceless this may not be the only difference between them, as we shall see later.

Immediately above the larynx is a space behind the tongue and reaching up towards the nasal cavity: this space is called *the pharynx* /færɪŋks/.

2.2 The palate

The palate, as Figure 1 shows, forms the roof of the mouth and separates the mouth cavity from the nose (or nasal) cavity. Make the tip of your tongue touch as much of your own palate as you can: most of it is hard and fixed in position, but when your tongue-tip is as far back as it will go, away from your teeth, you will notice that the palate becomes soft. Figure 3 is a more detailed view of the palate.

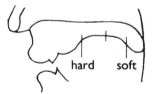

Fig. 3 The soft and hard parts of the palate

You can easily see the soft part of the palate if you use a mirror: turn your back to the light, open your mouth wide and say the vowel /ɑː/, and move the mirror so that the light shines into your mouth. You will be able to see the soft palate curving down towards the tongue and becoming narrower as it does so until it ends in a point called *the uvula* /juːvjʊlə/. Behind the soft palate you will be able to see part of the back wall of the pharynx. The soft palate can move: it can be raised so that it makes a firm contact with the back wall of the pharynx (as in Figure 3), and this stops the breath from going up into the nasal cavity and forces it to go into the mouth only. You can see this raising of the soft palate in your mirror if you keep your mouth wide open in position for the vowel /ɑː/ and push out your breath very fast, as if you were trying to blow out a match, still with your mouth open wide. You will see the soft palate move quickly upwards so that the breath all comes out of the mouth and none of it goes up into the nasal cavity. And when you relax after this the soft palate will come down again into its lowered position, shown in Figure 4.

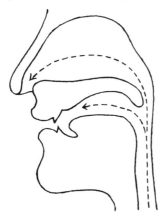

Fig. 4 *The soft palate lowered*

In this lowered position, the soft palate allows the breath to pass behind itself and up into the nasal cavity and out through the nose, as the dotted line shows. This is the normal position of the soft palate when we are not speaking but breathing quietly through the nose, with our mouth closed. It is also the position for the /m/-, /n/- and /ŋ/-sounds; say a long /m/-sound and nip your nose; this will stop the breath moving, and when you release it, the breath will continue out in a normal /m/-sound. Keep your lips closed and blow breath (without voice) hard through your nose, then draw it in again sharply: this will give you the feeling of breath moving in and out behind the soft palate.

Now say a /p/ but don't open your lips, just hold the breath behind the lips: there is no sound at all; keep your lips firmly closed still and send all the breath sharply out of the nose. Do this several times without opening your lips at all. What you feel at the back of your mouth is the soft palate going up and down; it is raised whilst you hold the /p/ and lowered suddenly when you let the air rush out through your nose.

The palate

For most of the sounds of all languages the soft palate is raised, so that the air is forced to go out through the mouth only.

Apart from this important raising and lowering of the soft palate, the whole of the palate, including the soft palate, is used by the tongue to interfere with the air stream. Say the vowel /ɑː/ again and watch the tongue in your mirror: it is flat in the mouth. Now add a /k/ after the /ɑː/ and you will see the back part of your tongue rise up and touch the soft palate so that the breath is completely stopped; then when you lower your tongue the breath rushes out again.

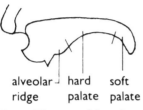

alveolar ridge — hard palate — soft palate

Fig. 5 The parts of the palate

The hard, fixed part of the palate is divided into two sections, shown in Figure 5, *the alveolar ridge* /ælvɪəʊlə rɪdʒ/ and *the hard palate*. The alveolar ridge is that part of the gums immediately behind the upper front teeth, and the hard palate is the highest part of the palate, between the alveolar ridge and the beginning of the soft palate. You can touch the whole of the alveolar ridge and the hard palate with your tongue-tip. The alveolar ridge is especially important in English because many of the consonant sounds like /t d n l r s z ʃ ʒ tʃ dʒ/ are made with the tongue touching or close to the alveolar ridge.

Finally the palate curves downwards towards the teeth at each side.

2.3 The teeth

The lower front teeth are not important in speech except that if they are missing certain sounds, e.g. /s/ and /z/, will be difficult to make. But the two upper front teeth are used in English to some extent. Put the tip of your tongue very close to the edge of these teeth and blow: this will produce a sound like the English /θ/ in *thin*; if you turn on the voice during this /θ/-sound you will get a sound like the English /ð/ in *this*.

2.4 The tongue

The tongue is the most important of the organs of speech because it

The speech organs

has the greatest variety of movement. Although the tongue has no obvious natural divisions like the palate, it is useful to think of it as divided into four parts, as shown in Figure 6.

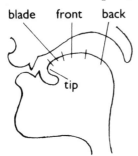

Fig. 6 The parts of the tongue

The *back* of the tongue lies under the soft palate when the tongue is at rest; the *front* lies under the hard palate, the *tip* and the *blade* lie under the alveolar ridge, the tip being the most forward part of all and the blade between the tip and the front. The tip and blade are particularly mobile and, as we have seen, they can touch the whole of the lips, the teeth, the alveolar ridge and the hard palate. The front can be flat on the bottom of the mouth or it can be raised to touch the hard palate, or it can be raised to any extent between these two extremes. Say the vowel /ɑː/ again and look into your mirror: the front is flat on the bottom of the mouth; now say /æ/ as in *cat*: the front rises a little; now say /e/ as in *met* (still keep your mouth as wide open as you can): the front rises again; and if you go on to say /iː/ as in *see* you will see that the front rises to a very high position, so high that it is hidden behind the teeth. These positions are shown in Figure 7. For /iː/ the front of

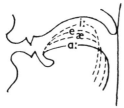

Fig. 7 Tongue positions for /iː, e, æ, ɑː/

the tongue comes very close to the hard palate. Put your mouth in this position, for /iː/, and draw air *inwards* quickly; you will feel cold air on the front of the tongue and on the hard palate just above it.

The tongue

The back of the tongue too can be flat in the mouth, or it can be raised to touch the soft palate, or it can be raised to any position between these two extremes. Say /ɑːk/ again, as you did earlier, and hold the /k/-sound with your mouth wide open. You will see in your mirror that the back of the tongue rises from a very flat position for ɑː to a position actually touching the soft palate for the /k/. Figure 8 shows these two extreme positions. The back of the tongue is in various positions between these two extremes for the vowels /ɒ, ɔː, ʊ, uː/ in *pot, fought, put, boot;* say them in that order and feel the back of the tongue rise gradually towards the soft palate: you will not be able to

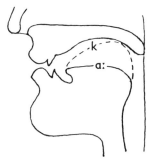

Fig. 8 Tongue positions for /ɑː, k/

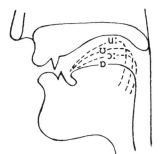

Fig. 9 Tongue positions for /uː, ʊ, ɔː, ɒ/

see the movement in the mirror because the lips will be in the way, but the position of the back of the tongue for each of these vowels is shown in Figure 9. In /uː/ the back of the tongue is very close to the soft palate; put your mouth in position for /uː/ and draw air *inwards* quickly: you will feel cold air on the back of the tongue and the soft palate. Now do the same for /iː/ again and feel the difference when the front of the tongue is raised. Go from the /iː/ position to the /uː/ position several

The speech organs

times whilst drawing breath inwards, and get used to this difference between a high front and a high back position.

The tongue can also change its shape in another way. Say the sound /s/, keep your mouth in the /s/ position and draw breath inwards; you will feel cold air passing through a narrow passage between the blade of the tongue and the alveolar ridge, but no cold air at the sides of the tongue. Now say an /l/-sound and draw air inwards. This time you will feel cold air passing between the *sides* of the tongue and the sides of the palate, but not down the centre of the tongue. This is because for /s/ the sides of the tongue are pressed firmly against the sides of the palate, so that the breath is forced to pass down the narrow central passage between the blade of the tongue and the alveolar ridge. In /l/ the centre of the mouth is blocked by the tip and blade of the tongue pressed firmly against the alveolar ridge and the air passes instead between the sides of the tongue and the sides of the palate. So the sides of the tongue may be either curved upwards to meet the sides of the palate or left flat so that they do not touch the sides of the palate. Open your mouth wide, use your mirror and try to make your tongue take up a flat shape, as in Figure 10, and then a curved shape, with the sides raised but the centre line lower, as in Figure 11. This last position is very important

Fig. 10 Front view of flat tongue

Fig. 11 Front view of grooved tongue

for English because many of the consonant sounds are pronounced with the sides of the tongue curved up in this way to meet the sides of the palate.

2.5 The lips

It is obvious that the lips can take up various different positions. They can be brought firmly together as in /p/ or /b/ or /m/ so that they completely block the mouth; the lower lip can be drawn inward and slightly upwards to touch the upper front teeth as in the sounds /f/ and /v/. And they can be kept apart either flat or with different amounts of rounding, and they can be pushed forward to a greater or lesser extent.

Of course, the closed position for /p, b, m/ and the lip-teeth position for /f/ and /v/ are used in English, but apart from this the English do not move their lips with very much energy: their lips are never very far apart, they do not take up very rounded shapes, they are rarely spread very much and almost never pushed forward or protruded. Watch English people talk either in real life or on films and notice how little the lips and the lower jaw move; some people make more lip-movement than others, but it is never necessary to exaggerate these movements. Watch people talking your language too, and see whether they move their lips more than the English. If so, you must remember when talking English to use your lips less than you do in your own language. The same is true for movements of the jaw: in normal speech there is rarely more than half an inch between the lips or a quarter of an inch between the teeth even when the mouth is at its widest open. No wonder English can be spoken quite easily whilst holding a pipe between the teeth!

In the chapters which follow we shall see how the movements of the organs of speech combine together in forming the sounds of English. You should study the descriptions of the movements very carefully, because what seems a quite small difference may in fact be very important in producing and recognizing an English sound correctly, and the difference between an English sound and one in your language may seem quite small when it is described, but the small difference in the movement of the speech organs may make all the difference between a result which sounds English and one which does not.

Suppose, for example, that in your language you have a /t/-sound which is made by touching the upper front teeth with the tip of your tongue: this is quite often the case. The difference between this /t/ and the /t/-sound of English is that the English /t/ is generally made with the tip of the tongue touching the alveolar ridge just behind the teeth. This may not seem much of a difference to you, but a /t/ which is made on the teeth sounds foreign to an English ear, and although it will be recognized as /t/, it will not sound correct in English.

The speech organs

When you study the movements of the speech organs for a certain sound of English, try to compare them with the movements for a similar sound in your language. Try to become conscious of what your speech organs are doing. The exercises which follow will help you to do this.

2.6 Exercises

(Answers, where appropriate, on p. 134)

1. Copy Figures 1, 3 and 6. Label all the different parts of the speech organs. Do this several times, until you can do it without looking at the book.
2. Three different actions take place in the larynx. What are they?
3. Which sounds in your language are voiced, and which are voiceless? Which of these sounds are similar except for a difference of voicing, like /s/ and /z/ in English?
4. Can you sing a voiceless sound? And if not, why not?
5. How does the soft palate affect the direction of the air stream?
6. What sounds in your language are made with the soft palate lowered?
7. Make a /p/-sound and hold it with the lips closed; then, still keeping the lips closed, let the air burst out through the nose. Do the same with /t/ and /k/. Do the same with /b, d/, and /g/ and let *voiced* air burst out through the nose.
8. Say several /k/-sounds quickly one after the other, /k-k-k-k-k/, and feel the back of the tongue touching and leaving the soft palate. Do the same with /t/ – first with the tongue touching the alveolar ridge; then with the tongue-tip touching the upper front teeth. Can you do the same thing with the tongue-tip touching the centre of the hard palate?
9. Make the vowels /iː, ɪ, e, æ/ and feel how the front of the tongue is lowered each time and the jaw opens gradually. Do the same with /uː, ʊ, ɔː, ɒ, ɑː/ and feel how the back of the tongue is lowered.
10. What does the tongue do in making the sounds /aɪ, ɔɪ, aʊ/?
11. Make the flat and curved shapes of the tongue shown in Figures 10 and 11. Use your mirror.
12. Make a /t/-sound and hold it with the tongue-tip in contact with the alveolar ridge. Now gently bring the teeth together. What happens to the sides of the tongue and why?
13. Put your mouth in an /l/ position and draw breath in and out. Feel

Exercises

it on the sides of the tongue. Do the same with /s/ and feel it on the centre of the tongue. Alternate the /s/ and /l/ positions and feel the sides of the tongue rise and lower as you go from one to the other.

3 The consonants of English

There are two good reasons for beginning with consonants rather than vowels. First, consonants contribute more to making English understood than vowels do. Second, consonants are generally made by a definite interference of the vocal organs with the air stream, and so are easier to describe and understand.

The sentence 'C—ld y— p-ss m- - p—c- -f str-ng, pl—s-' is easy for an English reader to understand even though all of the vowel *letters* have been left out. Similarly, if in actually speaking we could leave out all the vowel *sounds* and pronounce only the consonants most English would still be fairly easy to understand. But look at the same sentence with all the consonant letters left out: '-ou-- -ou -a-- -e a -ie-e o- —-i—, —ea-e.' It is impossible to make any sense out of it, and the same would be true in speaking, because the consonants form the bones, the skeleton of English words and give them their basic shape.

Native speakers of English from different parts of the world have different accents, but the differences of accent are mainly the result of differences in the sound of the *vowels;* the consonants are pronounced in very much the same way wherever English is spoken. So if the vowels you use are imperfect it will not prevent you from being understood, but if the consonants are imperfect there will be a great risk of misunderstanding.

In dealing with the consonants you must first learn how each one is mainly distinguished from the others, the features which it *must* have so that it will not be mistaken for any other consonant. Then later you will learn about any special sounds of that phoneme which need small changes in their formation in different circumstances, changes which are not essential if you simply want to be understood, but which will make your English sound better.

3.1 Friction consonants

There are nine consonant phonemes whose main sounds all have friction as their most important feature. They are /f, v, θ, ð, s, z, ʃ, ʒ, h/.

Friction consonants

For all of them the lungs push air through a narrow opening where it causes friction of various kinds.

/f/ and /v/

For both /f/ and /v/ the speech organs are in the position shown in Figure 12.

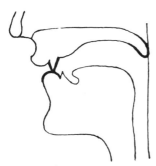

Fig. 12 /f/ and /v/

NOTICE
1 The soft palate is raised so that no air goes through the nose and it is all forced through the mouth.
2 The bottom lip is very close to the upper front teeth: this forms the narrowing and when air is pushed through this narrowing it causes slight friction.
3 The tongue is not directly concerned in making these sounds, but it does not lie idle; it takes up the position necessary for the *following* sound, so in fi: it will be in the /i:/ position whilst /f/ is being pronounced, and in fri: it will be in the /r/ position, and so on.

The difference between /f/ and /v/ is mainly one of *strength*: /f/ is a strong consonant, /v/ is a weak one. Also /f/ is never voiced, but /v/ may be. And /f/ is rather *longer* than /v/.
So /f/ is a strong, voiceless, long consonant, /v/ is a weak, perhaps voiced, short consonant.
Put your lower lip and upper teeth close together and blow breath between them quite strongly: continue the sound and listen to the friction – it is not very noisy but can be heard quite easily. Now blow the breath through very gently; the friction is much less and must *always* be much less for /v/ than for /f/. Alternate this strong and weak friction for /f/ and /v/; don't worry about voicing, it is not important.

Now say the word *fast* **faːst** with strong friction for the /f/. Now say *vast* **vaːst** with very short weak friction for the /v/. Alternate these: **faːst, vaːst**, and be sure that there is very little, very weak friction for the /v/, but also be sure that it is the lip and the teeth which are causing the friction, *not* the two lips. Keep the upper lip out of the way altogether.

If your language has both /f/ and /v/, the sounds that you use will probably do quite well in English, provided that you are quite sure that both of them have this lip-teeth action, especially the /v/. Although there is very little friction for /v/ there must always be some; it must not be completely frictionless. Now practise the following lists of words, with long, strong friction for /f/ and short, weak friction for /v/.

faːst	fast	vaːst	vast	fjuː	few	vjuː	view
fiːl	feel	viːl	veal	fɪə	fear	vɪə	veer
fəʊl	foal	vəʊl	vole	faɪl	file	vaɪl	vile
ferɪ	ferry	verɪ	very	fæt	fat	væt	vat
fæn	fan	væn	van	feɪl	fail	veɪl	veil

Now try these sounds between vowels. In this position the /v/ will be voiced in English, but the important thing for you is to make it short and weak: if you do this the voicing can take care of itself. (If your language has voiced /v/ anyway, this is fine.) Take special care in this position that the /v/ has some friction, though not too much, and that the friction is caused by lip-teeth action and not by the two lips. Use your mirror to make sure that the upper lip is well clear of the lower one.

sʌfə	suffer		kʌvə	cover
defə	deafer		nevə	never
snɪfɪŋ	sniffing		gɪvɪŋ	giving
pruːfɪŋ	proofing		pruːvɪŋ	proving
rʌfə	rougher		lʌvə	lover
səʊfə	sofa		əʊvə	over
seɪfə	safer		seɪvə	savour
ɒfə	offer		hɒvə	hover
dɪfaɪd	defied		dɪvaɪd	divide
rɪfjuːz	refuse		rɪvjuːz	reviews

In phrases we do exactly the same, long strong friction for /f/ and short weak friction for /v/. Try these:

Friction consonants

verɪ fɑːst	very fast	verɪ vɑːst	very vast
aɪ fiːl faɪn	I feel fine	aɪ fiːl vaɪl	I feel vile
faɪn fɜːz	fine furs	faɪn vɜːs	fine verse
fɔː fænz	four fans	fɔː vænz	four vans
ə gʊd fjuː	a good few	ə gʊd vjuː	a good view

When /f/ and /v/ occur at the end of words, after a vowel, they have an effect on the *length* of the vowel. The strong consonant /f/ makes the vowel shorter, the weak consonant /v/ makes the vowel longer. This is an important general rule which applies to many other pairs of consonants as well: *strong consonants at the end of words shorten the preceding vowel, weak consonants lengthen it.* In the words *safe* seɪf and *save* seɪv, the /f/ and the /v/ have the same features as before: /f/ is stronger and longer, /v/ is weaker and shorter, very short indeed in this position, but the vowels are of very different lengths; in seɪf the /eɪ/ is quite short and in seɪv it is really long.

Say these words, seɪf and seɪv, and be particularly careful to lengthen out the vowel in seɪv, drawl it, drag it out, and then add a very short weak /v/ friction at the very end. Don't shorten the /eɪ/ in seɪf *too* much, but do be sure that the /eɪ/ in seɪv is very much longer. Now do the same with the following words:

liːf	leaf	liːv	leave	laɪf	life	laɪv	live
hɑːf	half	hɑːv	halve	straɪf	strife	straɪv	strive
kɑːf	calf	kɑːv	carve	reɪf	Ralph	reɪv	rave
pruːf	proof	pruːv	prove	weɪf	waif	weɪv	wave
sɜːf	surf	sɜːv	serve	seɪf	safe	seɪv	save

These words all contain vowel phonemes which are naturally long, that is to say longer than the vowels /ɪ e æ ɒ ʊ ʌ/ in similar positions. The short vowels behave like the long ones when followed by /f/ or /v/, that is, they are shortest when followed by strong /f/ and rather longer when followed by weak /v/, although they are never so long as the long vowels when these are followed by the weak consonant.

Try this with the words below: before /f/ make the vowel quite short, and before /v/ make it a little longer, about as long as the long vowels before /f/. And still make /f/ longer and stronger, and /v/ very short and weak in friction.

stɪf	stiff	sɪv	sieve	ɒf	off	ɒv	of
klɪf	cliff	lɪv	live	rʌf	rough	dʌv	dove
snɪf	sniff	gɪv	give	blʌf	bluff	lʌv	love
gæf	gaffe	hæv	have	flʌf	fluff	glʌv	glove

Consonants

Now look at the phrases below, and decide which of the vowels have to be longer and which shorter. Remember that there are *three* lengths: (1) short vowels (/ɪ e æ ɒ ʊ ʌ/) before the strong consonant, e.g. stɪf, (2) short vowels before the weak consonant, *and* long vowels before the strong consonant, e.g. glʌv and weɪf, (3) long vowels before the weak consonant, e.g. seɪv. Now say them with good vowel length and good difference between /f/ and /v/.

ə hɑːf snɪf	a half sniff	ə breɪv blʌf	a brave bluff
ə stɪf glʌv	a stiff glove	ə laɪv dʌv	a live dove
ə briːf lʌv	a brief love	ə seɪf muːv	a safe move
ə rʌf greɪv	a rough grave	ə greɪv griːf	a grave grief
ə dwɔːf stəʊv	a dwarf stove	ə klɪf draɪv	a cliff drive

Some of the most common English words which contain /f/ are: *family, far, fat, father, feel, few, fried, first, for, four, five, from, friend, front, before, after, afraid, different, difficult, left, office, perfect, prefer, suffer, awful, often, half, off, knife, life, laugh, self, wife, safe, cough, rough, stiff.*

Some of the most common English words which contain /v/ are: *very, valve, visit, voice, value, violent, vast, van, view, ever, never, over, river, seven, several, travel, even, every, heavy, live, of, give, love, move, prove, receive, believe, save, serve, twelve, wave, five, have.*

Sometimes when you are listening to English, listen especially for these words (and others containing /f/ and /v/) and try to fix the sounds in your mind.

/θ/ and /ð/

/θ/ and /ð/ are also friction sounds, /θ/ is *strong* and /ð/ is *weak*. Both have the position of the speech organs shown in Figure 13.

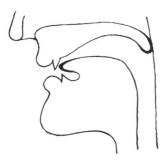

Fig. 13 /θ/ *and* /ð/

Friction consonants

NOTICE
1 The soft palate is raised so that all the breath is forced to go through the mouth.
2 The tip of the tongue is close to the upper front teeth: this is the narrowing where the friction is made.
3 The noise made by the friction for /θ/ and /ð/ is not very great, much less than for /s/ and /z/.

Put the tip of your tongue close to the cutting-edge of your upper front teeth. In a mirror you will be able to see the tip. Blow air through this position so that you get some friction, but not too much, not so much as for /s/. Continue the sound and listen to it. /θ/ should make the same amount of noise as /f/, not more. Try /f/ and /θ/ alternately until you get the friction right for /θ/. Now make less friction for /ð/ by pushing the air more gently. The friction for /ð/ when it is properly made can only just be heard. Now alternate the stronger /θ/ and the weaker /ð/ – not too much friction in /θ/ and even less in /ð/.

All that I said about strong and weak consonants on p. 25 is true for /θ/ and /ð/. /θ/ is stronger and longer and always voiceless, /ð/ is weaker and shorter and may be voiced. Confusing /θ/ and /ð/ will scarcely ever lead to misunderstanding because they rarely occur in words which are otherwise similar, but if you do not make the difference properly it will be noticeable.

Try the words given below, and be sure (1) that the air passes between the tongue tip and the teeth, and (2) that the friction is never too strong.

θɪn thin	ðen then	θæŋk thank	ðæt that
θɪŋk think	ðɪs this	θɔ:t thought	ðəʊz those
θi:f thief	ði:z these		

Some people may confuse /θ/ with /f/ and /ð/ with /v/; this is not very important for understanding, since some English speakers do the same, but you should try not to make these confusions because they will be noticeable. Say these words, and be sure that for /f/ and /v/ you are using a lip-teeth action, and for /θ/ and /ð/ a tongue-teeth action.

fɪn fin	θɪn thin	fɔ:t fought	θɔ:t thought
fri: free	θri: three	frɪl frill	θrɪl thrill
fɜ:st first	θɜ:st thirst	fɔ:tɪ forty	θɜ:tɪ thirty
ðæt that	væt vat	ðen then	vent vent
ðeɪ they	veɪn vain	ðeə there	vɪə veer
ði:z these	vi:l veal	ðəʊ though	vəʊt vote

Consonants

Between vowels /ð/ is voiced, but the important thing for you is to make it very short and weak, and let the voicing take care of itself. /θ/ is always voiceless. Say these words:

ɔ:θə	author	ʌðə	other	mɑ:θə	Martha	mʌðə	mother
ɑ:θə	Arthur	rɑ:ðə	rather	nʌθɪŋ	nothing	brʌðə	brother
ɜ:θɪ	earthy	wɜ:ðɪ	worthy	bɜ:θə	Bertha	fɜ:ðə	further

Now try to keep /f, v, θ, ð/ separate in this position.

ɔ:θə	author	ɒfə	offer	ɑ:θə	Arthur	tʌfə	tougher
nʌθɪŋ	nothing	pʌfɪŋ	puffing	tu:θɪ	toothy	ru:fɪŋ	roofing
brʌðə	brother	lʌvə	lover	leðə	leather	nevə	never
fɑ:ðə	father	kɑ:və	carver	hi:ðən	heathen	i:vən	even

At the end of words /θ/ and /ð/ affect a preceding vowel in the same way as /f/ and /v/. Try with some long vowels, and make the vowel specially long before /ð/.

grəʊθ	growth	ləʊð	loathe
tu:θ	tooth	smu:ð	smooth
bəʊθ	both	kləʊð	clothe
ri:θ	wreath	bri:ð	breathe
feɪθ	faith	beɪð	bathe
maʊθ	mouth (n.)	maʊð	mouth (vb.)

The only word in which /ð/ occurs finally after a short vowel is /wɪð/ *with*, but try keeping the vowel at its shortest in the following:

mɒθ	moth	mɪθ	myth	breθ	breath
deθ	death	rɒθ	wrath		

Some of the most common English words which contain /θ/ are: *thank, thick, thin, thing, thirsty, thousand, three, through, throw, Thursday, thought, thirty, healthy, wealthy, something, anything, both, bath, breath, cloth, earth, fourth,* etc., *faith, health, month, north, south, path, worth, death.*

Some of the most common English words which contain /ð/ (and some of these are amongst the commonest in the language) are: *the, this, that, these, those, there, their, then, they, them, though, than, other, mother, father, brother, either, neither, further, clothes, leather, together, weather, whether, breathe, with, smooth.*

Sometimes when you listen to English listen specially for these

Friction consonants

words (and others containing /θ/ and /ð/) and try to fix the sounds in your mind.

On p. 33 you will find more about /θ/ and /ð/ when they are close to /s/ and /z/.

/s/ and /z/

/s/ is a strong friction sound and /z/ is a weak one. The position of the speech organs for these sounds is shown in Figure 14.

NOTICE
1 The soft palate is raised so that all the breath is forced to go through the mouth.
2 The tip and blade of the tongue are very close to the alveolar ridge. There is a very considerable narrowing at this point, *not* near the teeth and *not* near the hard palate.
3 The teeth are very close together.
4 The friction for these sounds, especially for /s/, is much greater than for /f, v, θ/ and /ð/.

There will be a sound similar to /s/ in your language: make this sound, then keep your mouth in that position and draw air inwards; make small changes in the position of the tip and blade of the tongue until you can feel that the cold air is hitting the tongue at the very centre of the alveolar ridge, not further forward and not further back. /z/ is the weak sound, so when you are satisfied with the strong friction for /s/, push air through more slowly so that the friction is weaker. Alternate strong and weak friction.

Once again, as for the other consonants, the strong one, /s/, is longer and always voiceless, the weak one, /z/, is quite short and may be voiced, but again the *gentleness* of /z/ is the thing to concentrate on.

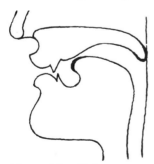

Fig. 14 /s/ *and* /z/

Consonants

/z/ is not a common sound at the beginning of words, so confusing /s/ and /z/ in initial position will not generally lead to misunderstanding; but English speakers do distinguish them, so you should try to do so too. Try the following words:

sɪŋk sink	zɪŋk zinc	suː Sue	zuː zoo
sed said	zed Zed	siːl seal	ziːl zeal
sɔːn sawn	zəʊn zone	sɪst cyst	zest zest

Between vowels /z/ is voiced, and if you voice this sound naturally in that position that is good; if not, the sound should be made very gently and very short. /s/ is always voiceless. Try these words:

luːsə looser	luːzə loser	kɔːsə coarser	kɔːzə causer
leɪsɪ lacy	leɪzɪ lazy	fʌsɪ fussy	fʌzɪ fuzzy
bʌsɪz buses	bʌzɪz buzzes	reɪsɪŋ racing	reɪzɪŋ raising

At the end of words, after a vowel, /s/ makes the vowel rather shorter and /z/ makes it longer, as with /f, v, θ, ð/, and in this position /z/ is particularly short and gentle – just the faintest touch of a /z/ is sufficient, but the vowel must be good and long. Try the words below and make both the difference of vowel length and of consonant strength:

pleɪs place	pleɪz plays	niːs niece	niːz knees
kɔːs coarse	kɔːz cause	praɪs price	praɪz prize
luːs loose	luːz lose	hɜːs hearse	hɜːz hers

And now some more with short vowels:

bʌs bus	bʌz buzz	hɪs hiss	hɪz his
æs ass	æz as		

For the speakers of many languages (e.g. French, German, Italian, Chinese, Japanese, Russian, etc.) there are not separate phonemes /θ/ and /s/ but only one which is usually more like the English /s/. So there is a danger that /s/ will be used instead of /θ/. The difference between them is that /s/ is made with the tip and blade of the tongue close to the centre of the alveolar ridge and makes a strong friction, whereas /θ/ is made with the tongue tip near the upper teeth and makes much less friction.

Distinguish carefully between all these pairs:

sɪn sin	θɪn thin	sɔːt sort	θɔːt thought
sɪŋ sing	θɪŋ thing	sʌm sum	θʌm thumb
sɪŋk sink	θɪŋk think	saɪ sigh	θaɪ thigh

Friction consonants

Now do them again, and be absolutely certain that you do not replace /s/ by /θ/: there is always a danger of replacing the more familiar with the less familiar sound, as well as the reverse.

Now try them at the end of words (the vowel length is the same all the time because both are strong consonants and shorten the vowel), but /s/ must still make much more noise than /θ/.

maʊs	mouse	maʊθ	mouth	feɪs	face	feɪθ	faith
mɒs	moss	mɒθ	moth	pɑːs	pass	pɑːθ	path
fɔːs	force	fɔːθ	fourth	wɜːs	worse	wɜːθ	worth

Repeat this exercise and be sure again that you are not replacing /s/ by /θ/.

The same difficulty applies to /z/ and /ð/. Both are weak sounds but /z/ makes more noise than /ð/. Try these words:

zuː	zoo	ðəʊ	though
briːz	breeze	briːð	breathe
raɪz	rise	raɪð	writhe
tiːzɪŋ	teasing	tiːðɪŋ	teething
riːzən	reason	hiːðən	heathen
zed	Zed	ðen	then
kləʊz	close	kləʊð	clothe
leɪz	lays	leɪð	lathe
kləʊzɪŋ	closing	kləʊðɪŋ	clothing
maɪzə	miser	naɪðə	neither

Go through these words again and be sure that you are not replacing /ð/ by /z/ or /z/ by /ð/.

Those people who speak languages where /θ/ and /s/ are not separate phonemes usually have a special difficulty when /s/ and /θ/ occur close together in words like θɪŋks *thinks*. Because /s/ and /θ/ are both made with the tongue-tip and because the teeth and the alveolar ridge are rather close together there is a danger of using /s/ in both places, or even /θ/ in both places, giving sɪŋks or θɪŋkθ. This must be avoided if possible. /z/ and /ð/ give exactly the same difficulty. Try the following words and be careful to make /s/ and /z/ noisy and /θ/ and /ð/ less noisy: saʊθ *south*, ðɪs *this*, ðiːz *these*, ðəʊz *those*, θaɪz *thighs*, smuːð *smooth*, θɪŋz *things*, sevənθ *seventh*, θɜːstɪ *thirsty*, mʌðəz *mothers*, sʌðən *southern*, ðeəz *theirs*, θɪsl̩ *thistle*.

Making /s, z/ and /θ, ð/ sufficiently different from each other is even more difficult when they are next to each other in a word or phrase like bɑːðz *baths* or bəʊθ saɪdz *both sides*. This happens very often in English because /s/ and /z/ are very common at the end of words and /ð/ begins some very common words such as *the, this, that, them,* etc.

Start with a long /θ/-sound, not too much noise, then slide the tip of the tongue gently backwards to the alveolar ridge, which will give the noisy /s/-sound. Do this several times, and be sure that you start with a good /θ/; then gradually make the /θ/ shorter before you slide the tip back to the /s/ position. Now practise these words and be careful to make a distinct difference each time:

mɒθ	moth	mɒs	moss	mɒθs	moths
mɪθ	myth	mɪs	miss	mɪθs	myths
fɔ:θ	fourth	fɔ:s	force	fɔ:θs	fourths

Now do the same with /ð/ and /z/; start with a long quiet /ð/ and gently slide the tongue back to give the noisier /z/. Gradually shorten the sounds (but be careful to make *both*, not /ð/ or /z/ alone) and then practise making a difference between these words:

bri:ð	breathe	bri:z	breeze	bri:ðz	breathes
raɪð	writhe	raɪz	rise	raɪðz	writhes
kləʊð	clothe	kləʊz	close	kləʊðz	clothes

Now try going from /s/ to /θ/; this time gently slide the tongue forward towards the teeth until the noisy /s/ is replaced by the quiet /θ/. Do this several times and be sure that *both* sounds are heard. Then practise these phrases:

ə naɪs θɪŋ	a nice thing		ɪts θɪk	it's thick
dʒæks θɪn	Jack's thin		lets θɪŋk	let's think
jes θæŋks	yes, thanks		pɑ:s θru:	pass through

Do the same with /z/ and /ð/ and then practise these phrases:

hu:z ðɪs	who's this?		ju:z ðæt	use that
əz ðəʊ	as though		dʒɒnz ðeə	John's there
lu:z ðəm	lose them		weəz ðə ti:	where's the tea?

And finally some more phrases in which /s, z, θ, ð/ come together in various orders. Always be careful to make one noisy sound (/s, z/) and one quiet one (/θ, ð/):

wɒts ðæt	what's that?		bəʊθ saɪdz	both sides
ɪts ðeəz	it's theirs		waɪz θɔ:ts	wise thoughts

Friction consonants

hiːz θɜːtɪ he's thirty	wɪð seɪftɪ with safety
briːð sɒftlɪ breathe softly	ðiːz θriː these three

There are various tongue-twisters – sentences which are difficult to say – based on the mixing of these four sounds; for example sɪks θɪn θɪs| stɪks *six thin thistle sticks* and ðə liːθ pəliːs dɪsmɪsəθ ʌs *the Leith police dismisseth us*, but native English speakers find these difficult to say, so there is no need to try to master them. It is much better to concentrate on words and phrases like those above which occur very often in normal conversation.

Some of the very many common words containing /s/ are: *same, sing, sit, Saturday, Sunday, save, see, say, second, seem, self, send, six, seven, side, since, sleep, slow, small, so, some, son, sister, soon, start, stay, stop, still, against, almost, beside(s), least, lost, last, listen, message, mister, Mrs, use* (n.), *face, miss, across, advice, case, cats* (etc.), *takes* (etc.), *pass, less, -ness, nice, piece, perhaps, yes.*

Some of the very many common words containing /z/ are: *noisy, busy, reason, easy, lazy, losing, as, his, hers, cause, use* (vb.), *has, is, lose, was, days, dogs* (etc.), *does, moves* (etc.), *noise, please.*

/ʃ/ and /ʒ/

/ʃ/ is a strong friction sound and /ʒ/ is a weak one. The position of the speech organs for these sounds is shown in Figure 15.

NOTICE
1 The soft palate is raised so that all the breath is forced to go through the mouth.
2 There is a narrowing between the tip of the tongue and the *back* of the alveolar ridge.
3 The *front* of the tongue is higher than for /s/ and /z/.
4 The lips are very slightly rounded.

Start from /s/: pull the tip of the tongue backwards a little so that the narrowing is at the back of the alveolar ridge (draw the breath inwards to check that you have the tongue in the right place). Keep this position and put the rest of the tongue in position to say the vowel /ɪ/, slightly round the lips, and push the breath through strongly. /ʃ/ is a much noisier sound than /f/ and /θ/ and only a little less noisy than /s/. For /ʒ/ the friction is weaker, and shorter.

/ʒ/ does not occur at the beginning of English words but /ʃ/ quite frequently does. Try these: ʃiː *she*, ʃəʊ *show*, ʃɒp *shop*, ʃɪp *ship*, ʃed *shed*,

Consonants

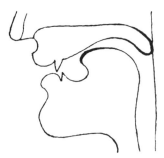

Fig. 15 /ʃ/ *and* /ʒ/

ʃɜːt *shirt*, ʃɑːp *sharp*, ʃɔːt *short*, ʃeə *share*, ʃaɪn *shine*, ʃʊə *sure*, ʃʌt *shut*, ʃuː *shoe*, ʃʊd *should*.

Between vowels /ʒ/ is voiced and if you voice this sound naturally in that position so much the better; if not, make it very gentle and very short. /ʃ/ is always voiceless. There are almost no cases in which /ʃ/ and /ʒ/ distinguish words which are otherwise the same, but practise these mixed words: preʃəs *precious*, treʒə *treasure*, əʊʃən *ocean*, ɪkspləʊʒən *explosion*, neɪʃən *nation*, ɪnveɪʒən *invasion*, kəndɪʃən *condition*, dɪsɪʒən *decision*, preʃə *pressure*, meʒə *measure*, rɪleɪʃən *relation*, əkeɪʒən *occasion*.

At the end of words /ʃ/ is quite common but /ʒ/ is very rare and only occurs in a few words borrowed from French: like the other gentle sounds it makes the vowel before it longer, whereas /ʃ/ makes it shorter. Try these /ʃ/ words:

fɪnɪʃ finish	rʌbɪʃ rubbish	kræʃ crash	krʌʃ crush
wɒʃ wash	pʊʃ push	liːʃ leash	hɑːʃ harsh

And now these /ʒ/ words, making the vowels fully long:

gærɑːʒ *garage*   beɪʒ *beige*   ruːʒ *rouge*

As you can see, if you confuse /ʃ/ and /ʒ/, not much damage is done, though since native English speakers distinguish them you should try to too. However, it is much more dangerous to confuse /s/ and /ʃ/ because many words are kept separate only by this difference. In some languages (e.g. Spanish, Greek) there is only one phoneme where English has both /s/ and /ʃ/ and if this is so you must take special care with these phonemes. (The replacement of /s/ by /ʃ/ gives a rather drunken effect to one's speech!) In particular the friction of /s/ is sharper and higher than that of /ʃ/ because the tongue-tip is nearer to

Friction consonants

the teeth, so practise the pairs of words below and be sure that you move your tongue to the right positions for the two consonants:

səʊ	so	ʃəʊ	show	saɪ	sigh	ʃaɪ	shy
sɒk	sock	ʃɒk	shock	siː	see	ʃiː	she
sɔːt	sort	ʃɔːt	short	seɪm	same	ʃeɪm	shame
pɜːsən	person	pɜːʃən	Persian	beɪsən	basin	neɪʃən	nation
lɪsən	listen	mɪʃən	mission	mɪsɪŋ	missing	wɪʃɪŋ	wishing
liːs	lease	liːʃ	leash	æs	ass	æʃ	ash
mes	mess	meʃ	mesh				

The danger of confusing words with /z/ and /ʒ/ is very small because few pairs of words have only this difference, but to use one of these where the other is usual will make your English sound wrong, so keep the two separate. Try the following:

rɪzən	risen	vɪʒən	vision	reɪzə	razor	ɪreɪʒə	erasure
reɪzən	raisin	ɪnveɪʒən	invasion	rəʊzə	Rosa	kləʊʒə	closure
ruːz	ruse	ruːʒ	rouge	beɪz	bays	beɪʒ	beige

Some of the commonest words containing /ʃ/ are: *shape, she, ship, sharp, shop, shall, should, short, shut, shout, show, shoulder, shoe, shoot, shine, shore, sure, anxious, ashamed, machine, patient, position, station, motion, nation, ocean, mention, pressure, precious, bush, crash, crush, fish, flesh, foolish, fresh, greenish* (etc.), *punish, push, rush, selfish, wash, wish, dish.*

Some of the commonest words containing /ʒ/ are: *measure, pleasure, usual, division, revision, collision, invasion, vision, inclusion, illusion, provision, explosion, leisure, garage, barrage, rouge, beige.*

/h/

There are as many /h/-sounds in English as there are vowels, because /h/ always occurs before a vowel and consists of the sound of breath passing between the open vocal cords and out of the mouth which is already prepared for the following vowel. Before /iː/ the mouth is in position for /iː/, before /ɑː/ it is ready for /ɑː/, and so on; so in order to make /h/-sounds, the mouth is held ready for the vowel and a short gasp of breath is pushed up by the lungs. /h/ does not make very much noise, but it must not be left out when it should be sounded, for two reasons: (1) many words are distinguished by the presence or absence of /h/, like hɪə *here* and ɪə *ear*, (2) English speakers consider that the leaving out of /h/ is the mark of an uncultivated speaker.

Consonants

Leaving out /h/ is the biggest danger, but a lesser error is to make /h/-sounds too noisy. Some speakers (for instance, Spaniards, Greeks, Poles) push the breath between the back of the tongue and the soft palate and make a scraping noise at that point. This sounds rather unpleasant to English people and you should avoid it if possible. For the words below, get your mouth ready for the vowel and push a little gasp of breath through your mouth just before the vowel starts:

| ha:t heart | hɜ: her | hæt hat |
| hɔ:l hall | hu: who | hi: he |

Say all those words several times and be sure that the /h/-sound is there, but not too noisy – just the sound of breath streaming from the mouth.

Now compare the following pairs, one word with /h/ and one without:

ha:m harm	a:m arm	hi:t heat	i:t eat
hedʒ hedge	edʒ edge	hɔ:l hall	ɔ:l all
heə hair	eə air	hɪl hill	ɪl ill

/h/ also occurs in the middle of words (although never at the end of words) and should be made in the same way as before. If the vocal cords happen to vibrate and give voice during /h/ this is normal, but there is no need to try especially to voice the sound. Try these words, with a definite /h/, but no scraping:

bɪhaɪnd behind	rɪhɜ:s rehearse	ri:haʊz re-house
enɪhaʊ anyhow	ki:həʊl key-hole	ʌnhəʊlɪ unholy
ælkəhɒl alcohol	bɪfɔ:hænd beforehand	

/h/ is especially difficult for those who have no such sound in their own language (for example French, Italian) in phrases where words with /h/ and words without it are close together. If you have this trouble you must practise examples like those below quite *slowly* at first, and be sure that the words which ought to have /h/ do actually have it, and, equally important, that those without /h/ do *not* have it. Try them now, slowly:

haʊz a:θə	how's Arthur?
aʊt əv hænd	out of hand
ɪt s ɔ:flɪ hevɪ	it's awfully heavy
hɪz həʊmz ɪn aɪələnd	his home's in Ireland
helən went aʊt	Helen went out

Friction consonants

wiː ɔːl went həʊm	we all went home
aɪ hɪt henrɪ ɪn ðiː aɪ	I hit Henry in the eye
aɪ ɑːskt æn haʊ ʃiː hɜːd əbaʊt ɪt	I asked Ann how she heard about it

Say each of those examples several times slowly with the /h/ in the right places before you speed up to a normal pace.

A few common words sometimes have /h/ and sometimes do not, for example, *he, him, her, have*. This is explained on p. 92.

Some of the commonest words which always contain /h/ are: *half, hand, hat, head, health, hear, here, heart, heavy, hide, high, history, hit, hold, hole, home, hope, horse, hat, house, how, hundred, husband, behind, beforehand, household, anyhow, greenhouse, manhole, inhale, rehearse, coherent.*

3.2 Stop consonants

In stop consonants the breath is completely stopped at some point in the mouth, by the lips or tongue-tip or tongue-back, and then released with a slight explosion. There are four pairs of phonemes containing stops /p, b/, /t, d/, /k, g/ and /tʃ, dʒ/, and like the friction consonants one of each pair is strong and the other weak.

/p/ and /b/

/p/ is a strong stop consonant and /b/ is a weak one. The position of the organs of speech for these stops is shown in Figure 16.

NOTICE
1 The lips are closed firmly and the soft palate is raised so that the breath cannot get out of either the nose or the mouth but is trapped for a short time.
2 When the lips are opened suddenly the breath rushes out with a slight explosion or popping noise.
3 Before the lips are opened, the rest of the mouth takes up the position for the following sound, a vowel position if a vowel follows, as in *pool*, or a consonant position if a consonant follows, as in *play*.

/p/ is a strong sound, like /f/ and /θ/ and /s/ and /ʃ/, but it has a special feature which these do not have: it causes the following sound to lose some of the voicing which it would otherwise have. For example, in puːl *pool* the first part of the vowel /uː/ has no voice – it consists of breath flowing through the mouth which is in position for /uː/. In fact this is what happens for /h/, as we saw on p. 37, so that we may write

Consonants

this voiceless period like this: pʰuːl, where the ʰ represents a voiceless kind of /uː/. Try making this voiceless /uː/ by itself; it is rather like what you do when you blow out a light. Now put the /p/ in front of it, still with no voice, only strong breath. Now put the vowel /uː/ itself after the breath, pʰuː. Do this several times and be sure that the period of breath is there before the /uː/ starts. Do the same thing with other vowels in the words pʰɔːt, pʰɑːt, pʰæt, pʰet, pʰɪt, pʰiːt. It is very

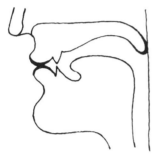

Fig. 16 /p/ *and* /b/

important that the period of breath (which is called *aspiration*) should be there each time. It is this aspiration which mainly separates /p/ from /b/.

Now try /p/ with a following consonant, as in /pleɪ/. Keep the lips closed for /p/, and behind them put your tongue in position for /l/; then open the lips and let the breath flow through the /l/ position, with no voice but considerable friction. This gives a voiceless /l/-sound, which is written /l̥/. Do this several times – pl̥, pl̥, pl̥ – still with no voice. Now put the ordinary voiced /l/ after pl̥ – pl̥l – and then go on to the vowel, pl̥leɪ. Do the same thing with the words preɪ and pjʊə, and see that breath flows through the /r/ and /j/ position, giving /r̥/ and /j̥/, with friction, before the voiced /r/ and /j/ are heard.

/b/ is a weak stop, and it *never* has aspiration. The vocal cords may or may not vibrate whilst the lips are still closed, but they must vibrate for the following sound, whether vowel or consonant. Try the word bʊk, and make the /b/ very gentle and without any aspiration. Do the same with bɔːt, bɑː, bæk, bel, bɪt, biːn. A following consonant is prepared for whilst the lips are closed and is voiced as soon as they open. Try braɪt, bluː, bjuːtɪ with a gentle /b/.

Now try the following pairs of words, and make the /p/ strong and aspirated and the /b/ weak and unaspirated:

Stop consonants

piːk peak	biːk beak	pɪt pit	bɪt bit
pæk pack	bæk back	paːk park	baːk bark
pɔːt port	bɔːt bought	pʊl pull	bʊl bull
praɪd pride	braɪd bride	pleɪz plays	bleɪz blaze

When /p/ occurs between vowels the aspiration may be less noticeable or even absent, but it will never do any harm to keep the aspiration in this position too. /b/ is of course never aspirated, but in this position it is usually voiced. The most important thing, as with the other weak consonants, is to make it very gentle and short. Try these words:

hæpɪ happy	ʃæbɪ shabby	sʌpə supper	rʌbə rubber
peɪpə paper	leɪbə labour	rɪpel repel	rɪbel rebel (vb.)
sɪmpl̩ simple	sɪmbl̩ symbol	əplaɪ apply	əblaɪdʒ oblige

Some learners (e.g. Spaniards) have great difficulty in hearing and making a difference between /b/ and /v/ in this position, so that the words *marble* and *marvel* sound the same. They must take great care to close the lips *very firmly* for /b/, so that the sound makes an explosion and not a friction. Try these words:

maːbl̩ marble	maːvl̩ marvel	rɪbən ribbon	rɪvə river
hæbɪt habit	hævɪt have it	rʌbə rubber	lʌvə lover
leɪbə labour	feɪvə favour	beɪbɪ baby	neɪvɪ navy

In final position (before a pause) /p/ is aspirated and shortens the vowel before it, whilst /b/ is particularly weak and makes only very little noise, but lengthens the vowel before it.

In some languages (e.g. Cantonese, Vietnamese) a final stop is not exploded or is replaced by a glottal stop (a stop consonant in which the breath is blocked by the vocal cords, see p. 14). Speakers of these languages must be very careful to form /p/ and /b/ with the lips, and to open the lips and allow the breath to explode out of the mouth before a pause. Try these words:

rɪp rip	rɪb rib	kæp cap	kæb cab
rəʊp rope	rəʊb robe	traɪp tripe	traɪb tribe
tæp tap	tæb tab	ræp wrap	græb grab

Those who have difficulty with /b/ and /v/ must again be sure to close the lips firmly for the /b/ and make a very light explosion but no friction. Try:

Consonants

rɪb	rib	gɪv	give	kæb	cab	hæv	have
traɪb	tribe	draɪv	drive	klʌb	club	glʌv	glove

When /p/ or /b/ are followed immediately by one of the other stop consonants /t, d, k, g/ or by /m/ or /n/ the sound is made a little differently; this is dealt with on p. 67.

Some of the commonest words containing /p/ are: *page, pair, paper, pardon, part, pass, pay, people, perhaps, piece, place, plate, play, please, plenty, poor, possible, post, pound, pretty, price, pull, push, put, appear, April, company, compare, complain, complete, copy, expect, happen, happy, important, open, sleep, cheap, cup, drop, group, heap, help, hope, keep, map, rope, shape, sharp, shop, stop, step, top, up, wrap.*

Some of the commonest words containing /b/ are: *back, bad, bag, bath, be, beautiful, because, become, bed, before, begin, behind, believe, belong, below, besides, best, between, big, black, blue, both, boy, bread, break, breakfast, bring, but, busy, buy, by, brown, able, about, above, September* (etc.), *February, habit, harbour, husband, neighbour, number, obey, possible, probable, public, remember, table, job, rub, rob, club, slab, grab.*

/t/ and /d/

/t/ is a strong stop consonant and /d/ is a weak one. The position of the organs of speech for these stops is shown in Figure 17.

NOTICE
1. The tip of the tongue (*not* the blade) is firmly against the middle of the alveolar ridge, not too near the teeth and not near the hard palate.
2. The soft palate is raised, so the breath cannot escape through either the nose or the mouth, but is trapped for a short time.
3. The sides of the tongue are firmly against the sides of the palate, so that the breath cannot pass over the sides of the tongue.
4. When the tongue-tip is lowered suddenly from the teeth ridge the breath rushes out with a slight explosion or popping noise.

The strong stop /t/ is aspirated in the same way as /p/ and this may be written in a similar way, e.g. tʰuː *too*. Put the tongue tip on the very centre of the alveolar ridge; be sure that only the very point of the tongue is in contact, not the blade; then allow the air to burst out with a voiceless vowel /uː/; do this several times before adding the normal voiced vowel and be sure that when you do add the /uː/ the voiceless period is still there. Do this several times and each time check the exact

Stop consonants

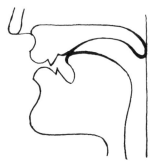

Fig. 17 /t/ and /d/

position of the tongue-tip and the aspiration. Then do the same thing with other vowels: tʰɔːt, tʰɒp, tʰɪn, tʰiː, tʰɜːn, tʰʌn. Then try the word twɪn, where the first part of /w/ comes out voiceless and tjuːn where /j/ is also partly voiceless.

/d/ is short and weak and never aspirated; compare the following words:

tuː	two	duː	do	tɔːn	torn	dɔːn	dawn
ten	ten	den	den	taɪ	tie	daɪ	die
tʌn	ton	dʌn	done	taʊn	town	daʊn	down
tjuːn	tune	djuːn	dune	twɪn	twin	dwɪndl̩	dwindle

As with /p/, when /t/ occurs between vowels, the aspiration may be weaker or even absent, but it will never do any harm to keep the aspiration in this position too. /d/ in this position is usually voiced, but concentrate mainly on making it very gentle and short, and if it is voiced as well so much the better. Try these words:

raɪtə	writer	raɪdə	rider	wetɪŋ	wetting	wedɪŋ	wedding
lætə	latter	lædə	ladder	wɔːtə	water	wɔːdə	warder
waɪtɪʃ	whitish	waɪdɪʃ	widish	pʊtɪŋ	putting	pʊdɪŋ	pudding

Speakers who find /b/ and /v/ difficult in this position will also find /d/ and /ð/ hard to distinguish. Concentrate on making /d/ with the tip of the tongue firmly against the alveolar ridge, and make sure it is a firm stop rather than a friction sound. Compare:

raɪdɪŋ	riding	raɪðɪŋ	writhing
briːdɪŋ	breeding	briːðɪŋ	breathing
ləʊdɪŋ	loading	ləʊðɪŋ	loathing
lædə	ladder	læðə	lather

Consonants

In final position /t/ is aspirated and shortens the vowel before it, whilst /d/ is particularly weak and makes only very little noise, but lengthens the vowel before it. However, speakers who tend not to allow /t/ and /d/ to explode in this position should be sure not only to make the difference of vowel length but also to allow the breath to explode out of the mouth. Try these words:

bet bet	bed bed	hɑːt heart	hɑːd hard
leɪt late	leɪd laid	saɪt sight	saɪd side
set set	sed said	brɔːt brought	brɔːd broad

/d/ and /ð/ may again be difficult to distinguish in this position. Be sure that /d/ is made with the tongue-tip firmly on the alveolar ridge, and that the breath is released with a tiny explosion. Try the words:

| briːd breed | briːð breathe | raɪd ride | raɪð writhe |
| ləʊd load | ləʊð loathe | saɪd side | saɪð scythe |

When /t/ and /d/ are followed by any of the other stop consonants, /p, b, k, g/ or by /m/ or /n/ or /l/, the sounds are made a little differently. This is dealt with on pp. 67–73.

Some of the many common words containing /t/ are: *table, take, tell, ten, time, to, today, together, too, top, towards, town, Tuesday, turn, twelve, two, talk, taste, after, better, between, city, dirty, hotel, into, matter, notice, particular, protect, quarter, Saturday, water, writer, about, at, beat, bite, boat, but, coat, eat, eight, fat, flat, gate, get, great, hot, it, let, lot, not, ought, might, put, what*. (Notice also the past tense of verbs ending with a strong consonant, e.g. *missed* mɪst, *laughed* lɑːft.)

Some of the many common words containing /d/ are: *day, dead, dear, December, decide, depend, different, difficult, do* (etc.), *dinner, dog, door, down, during, already, Monday* (etc.), *holiday, idea, lady, ladder, medicine, body, ready, shoulder, study, today, under, add, afraid, bad, bed, bird, could, would, end, friend, good, had, head, old, read, road, side*. (Notice also the past tense of verbs ending with a vowel, a weak consonant, and /t/, e.g. *owed* əʊd, *failed* feɪld, *started* stɑːtɪd.)

/k/ and /g/

/k/ is a strong stop consonant and /g/ is a weak one. The position of the organs of speech for these sounds is shown in Figure 18.

NOTICE

1 The back of the tongue is in firm contact with the soft palate, and

Stop consonants

the soft palate is raised, so that the breath is trapped for a short time.
2 When the tongue is lowered suddenly from the soft palate, the breath rushes out of the mouth with a slight explosion or popping noise.

The strong stop /k/ is aspirated in the same way as /p/ and /t/, and this may be shown in a similar way, e.g. kʰuːl *cool*. Put the tongue in position for /k/ and let the breath burst out in a voiceless /uː/. Do this several times before adding a normal vowel /uː/ after the voiceless one,

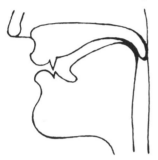

Fig. 18 /k/ and /g/

and be sure that the voiceless period, the aspiration, comes before the normal vowel each time. Then do the same thing with other vowels in: kʰɔːt, kʰɑːt, kʰæt, kʰɪl, kʰiːp. Now do the same thing with the following consonants in kliːn, kriːm, kwiːn, kjuː, where the first part of the /l, r, w/ and /j/ comes out voiceless.

The speakers of some languages (e.g. Greek, Persian) may form the stop too far forward in the mouth, with the front of the tongue against the hard palate, before the vowels /e/ and /æ/. This is not a very dangerous mistake, but to English ears the result sounds like /kje/ and/ kjæ/ rather than /ke/ and /kæ/, so that it should be avoided if possible. If you have this difficulty, say the words kʌt *cut* and kɑːt *cart* very slowly several times and notice carefully where the tongue touches the soft palate. Then try to keep this position in words such as kept *kept*, kemɪst *chemist*, kæt *cat* and kæn *can*.

/g/ is short and weak and never aspirated; compare the following words (and do not forget the aspiration of /k/):

keɪv	cave	geɪv	gave	kɑːd	card	gɑːd	guard
kɜːl	curl	gɜːl	girl	kʊd	could	gʊd	good
kæp	cap	gæp	gap	kəʊl	coal	gəʊl	goal
klɑːs	class	glɑːs	glass	krəʊ	crow	grəʊ	grow

Consonants

As with /p/ and /t/, when /k/ occurs between vowels the aspiration may be weaker or even absent, but it may be kept in this position too. On the other hand /g/ is normally voiced in this position (and of course never aspirated), but concentrate mainly on making it gentle and short. Speakers who confuse /b/ and /d/ with /v/ and /ð/ in this position will also tend to make /g/ a friction sound instead of the correct stop sound. They must be sure to put the tongue into firm contact with the palate and let the breath out with a definite, though slight, explosion. Try these words:

lıkıŋ	licking	dıgıŋ	digging	lækıŋ	lacking	lægıŋ	lagging
wiːkə	weaker	iːgə	eager	θıkə	thicker	bıgə	bigger
mɑːkɪt	market	tɑːgɪt	target	æŋkl̩	ankle	æŋgl̩	angle

In final position /k/ is aspirated and shortens the vowel before it, but /g/ is very, very gentle and lengthens the vowel before it. For both consonants there must be a definite explosion, a strong one for /k/ and a weak one for /g/; a closure without explosion or a simple friction is not correct. Try these words:

pɪk	pick	pɪg	pig	dɒk	dock	dɒg	dog
bæk	back	bæg	bag	lɒk	lock	lɒg	log
leɪk	lake	pleɪg	plague	brəʊk	broke	rəʊg	rogue

When /k/ and /g/ are followed by any of the other stop consonants, /p, b, t, d/, or by /m/ or /n/, the sounds are made a little differently. This is dealt with on pp. 67–73.

Some of the commonest words containing /k/ are: *call, can, car, care, carry, case, catch, cause, kind, kitchen, kill, coal, coat, cold, come, cook, corner, count, country, cup, cut, because, become, box, breakfast, excuse, pocket, second, secret, walking* (etc.), *weaker* (etc.), *local, ask, back, black, book, break, dark, drink, lake, like, lock, make, mistake, music, neck, o'clock, quick, take.*

Some of the commonest words containing /g/ are: *game, garden, gate, get, girl, glass, go, good, grass, great, green, grey, ground, grow, guess, gun, again, against, ago, agree, angry, August, exact, forget, language, regular, together, longer, bigger* (etc.), *tiger, begin, bag, beg, big, dog, fog, leg, rug, plug, flag, drug.*

/tʃ/ and /dʒ/

As the phonetic symbols suggest, /tʃ/ and /dʒ/ are stop consonants of a

Stop consonants

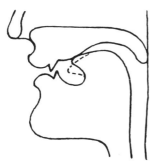

Fig. 19 /tʃ/ and /dʒ/

special kind. The air is trapped as for all the stop consonants, but it is released with definite friction of the /ʃ, ʒ/ kind. The position of the organs of speech for /tʃ/ and /dʒ/ is shown in Figure 19.

NOTICE

1 The tongue-tip touches the back part of the alveolar ridge, and the soft palate is raised so that the breath is trapped for a short time.
2 The rest of the tongue is in the /ʃ, ʒ/ position (see Figure 15).
3 The tongue-tip moves away from the alveolar ridge a little way (see the dotted lines in Figure 19), and the whole tongue is then in the /ʃ, ʒ/ position, so that a short period of this friction is heard. The friction of /tʃ/ and /dʒ/ is not so long as for /ʃ/ and /ʒ/ alone.

Start with /ʃ/: say a long /ʃ/ and then raise the tip of the tongue to the nearest part of the alveolar ridge and cut off the friction; then say /ʃ/ again by lowering the tongue-tip. Do this several times. Now start from the closed position, then release the tongue and say /ʃ/. This is /tʃ/. (English children imitate a steam engine by a series of /tʃ/-sounds.) Now try the word tʃiːp *cheap*, and don't make the /ʃ/ friction too long; it is rather shorter than in ʃiːp *sheep*. Like /ʃ/, /tʃ/ is a strong sound, whereas /dʒ/ is a weak one. Try /dʒ/ by making the friction very weak and shorter than for /tʃ/. Then try these words:

tʃɪn chin	dʒɪn gin	tʃəʊk choke	dʒəʊk joke
tʃɪə cheer	dʒɪə jeer	tʃeɪn chain	dʒeɪn Jane
tʃɔɪs choice	dʒɔɪs Joyce	tʃest chest	dʒest jest

Between vowels /dʒ/ is normally voiced, but the important thing is to keep it weak and to keep the friction short: if you also voice it, so much the better. /tʃ/ is still strong and voiceless. Try these words:

Consonants

rɪtʃɪz	riches	rɪdʒɪz	ridges
kætʃɪŋ	catching	kædʒɪŋ	cadging
fetʃɪŋ	fetching	edʒɪŋ	edging
bætʃɪz	batches	bædʒɪz	badges
wɒtʃɪŋ	watching	lɒdʒɪŋ	lodging
kɪtʃən	kitchen	pɪdʒən	pigeon

In final position /tʃ/ is still strong and voiceless, and it shortens the vowel before it; /dʒ/ is very weak and short, and it lengthens the vowel before it. Try these words:

rɪtʃ	rich	rɪdʒ	ridge	kætʃ	catch	kædʒ	cadge
sɜːtʃ	search	sɜːdʒ	surge	eɪtʃ	H	eɪdʒ	age
fetʃ	fetch	edʒ	edge	wɒtʃ	watch	lɒdʒ	lodge

There may be a danger for some speakers (e.g. Spaniards) of not distinguishing between /tʃ/ and /ʃ/, and between /dʒ/ and /ʒ/. These speakers must be careful to make a definite stop before the friction for /tʃ/ and /dʒ/, and no stop at all for /ʃ/ and /ʒ/. Practise with these words:

ʃuː	shoe	tʃuː	chew
wɒʃɪŋ	washing	wɒtʃɪŋ	watching
wɪʃ	wish	wɪtʃ	witch
leʒə	leisure	ledʒə	ledger
ʃɒp	shop	tʃɒp	chop
kæʃɪŋ	cashing	kætʃɪŋ	catching
kæʃ	cash	kætʃ	catch
meʒə	measure	meɪdʒə	major

Some of the commonest words containing /tʃ/ are: *chair, chance, change, cheap, chief, child, choice, choose, church, fortune, future, kitchen, nature, picture, question, catch, each, March, much, reach, rich, speech, stretch, such, teach, touch, watch, which.*

Some of the commonest words containing /dʒ/ are: *general, gentleman, January, join, joke, journey, joy, judge, July, jump, June, just, danger, imagine, soldier, subject, age, arrange, bridge, edge, language, large, manage, message, page, strange, village.*

3.3 Nasal consonants

There are three phonemes in English which are represented by nasal consonants, /m, n, ŋ/. In all nasal consonants the soft palate is lowered

Nasal consonants

and at the same time the mouth passage is blocked at some point, so that all the air is pushed out of the nose.

/m/ and /n/

All languages have consonants which are similar to /m/ and /n/ in English. The position of the speech organs for these sounds is shown in Figures 20 and 21.

NOTICE
1 The soft palate is lowered for both /m/ and /n/.
2 For /m/ the mouth is blocked by closing the two lips, for /n/ by pressing the tip of the tongue against the alveolar ridge, and the sides of the tongue against the sides of the palate.
3 Both sounds are voiced in English, as they are in other languages, and the voiced air passes out through the nose.

Neither of these sounds will cause much difficulty to most speakers. In many languages /n/ is made with the tongue-tip on the teeth themselves

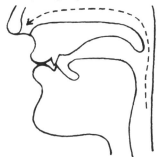

Fig. 20 /m/

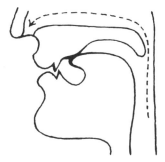

Fig. 21 /n/

rather than on the alveolar ridge, and this should be avoided if possible, but the use of a dental /n/ in English is hardly noticeable. Speakers of some languages (e.g. Portuguese, Yoruba) may have difficulty with these consonants in final position or before other consonants, for example in the words *can* kæn and *camp* kæmp. Instead of making a firm closure with the lips or tongue-tip so that all the breath goes through the nose, they may only lower the soft palate and *not* make a closure, so that some of the breath goes through the nose but the remainder goes through the mouth. When this happens we have a *nasalized vowel*. The word *can* would then be pronounced kæ̃, where æ̃ represents æ pronounced with the soft palate lowered, and *camp* would be kæ̃p. These speakers must be careful to close the lips firmly for /m/ and put the tongue-tip firmly in contact with the alveolar ridge for /n/ and be sure that the closure is completed every time one of these consonants occurs. Practise these words and make /m/ and /n/ rather long if you have this difficulty:

hɪm him	læm lamb	ruːm room	geɪm game
lɪmp limp	læmp lamp	lʌmp lump	geɪmz games
wʌn one	tɪn tin	suːn soon	maɪn mine
send send	sent sent	fɒnd fond	sʌnz sons

When /m/ or /n/ is found before another consonant, as in some of the examples above, the voiced or voiceless nature of the final consonant has an effect on the length of both the vowel *and* the nasal consonant: this is very similar to the lengthening or shortening of the vowel in examples like *seed/seat*. In the pairs of words below make the /m/ or /n/ quite long in the first word, before the gentle voiced consonant, and make it short in the second word, before the strong, voiceless consonant:

læmz	lambs	læmp	lamp
send	send	sent	sent
dʒɔɪnd	joined	dʒɔɪnt	joint
hʌmz	hums	hʌmp	hump
sɪnz	sins	sɪns	since
kəmpleɪnd	complained	kəmpleɪnt	complaint

/n/ is often syllabic: that is, it occupies the place at the centre of the syllable which usually is occupied by a vowel. Both the words *lesser* and *lesson* have two syllables: in *lesser* the second syllable is /-sə/, and in *lesson* the second syllable is often /-sn̩/ (/n̩/ means that /n/ is syllabic)

Nasal consonants

though the word may also be pronounced lesən, with a vowel *between* the /s/ and the /n/. This is true of all the following words, and you may pronounce them with or without the vowel before the /n/. If you leave out the vowel the /n/ will have the same length as the final vowel in lesə. Try these:

pɜːsn̩ person	riːzn̩ reason	iːvn̩ even	ɒfn̩ often
fæʃn̩ fashion	əkeɪʒn̩ occasion	riːdʒn̩ region	kɪtʃn̩ kitchen

In words such as *written, garden* a syllabic /n̩/ is almost always used immediately after the /t/ or /d/, that is rɪtn̩, gɑːdn̩. This requires a special pronunciation of /t/ and /d/ and is dealt with on p. 70.

English people sometimes pronounce a syllabic /m̩/ in words like *blossom, rhythm* blɒsm̩, rɪðm̩, but more often they are pronounced blɒsəm, rɪðəm, and that is what you should do.

Some of the commonest words containing /m/ are: *make, man, many, marry, matter, may, me, mean, meat, middle, mind, money, more, mouth, move, much, must, my, almost, among, common, complete, family, promise, remember, simple, summer, tomorrow, woman, am, arm, become, come, farm, form, from, him, home, room, same, seem, some, swim, them, time, warm, welcome.*

Some of the commonest words containing /n/ are: *name, near, nearly, need, neither, never, new, next, nice, night, nine, no, noise, nose, north, notice, now, number, know, knee, and, answer, any, behind, country, dinner, enough, finish, funny, general, journey, manner, many, penny, since, un-, went, winter, again, alone, been, begin, between, can, done, down, green, in, join, learn, on, one, rain, run, skin, son, soon, sun, -teen, ten, than, then.*

/ŋ/

This is the third English nasal consonant and the only one likely to cause trouble, because many languages do not have a consonant formed like /ŋ/. The position of the speech organs for /ŋ/ is shown in Figure 22.

NOTICE
1 The soft palate is lowered and all the air passes out through the nose.
2 The mouth is blocked by the back of the tongue pressed against the soft palate.
3 The sound is voiced.

Remember first of all that the letters *ng* in words like *sing* represent only

Consonants

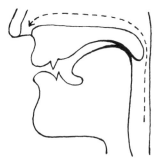

Fig. 22 /ŋ/

one sound for most English speakers: a few use two sounds and pronounce the word si**ŋg**, so if you do this it will be perfectly well understood and it is better to pronounce si**ŋg** than to confuse this word with si**n**. But it is better still to pronounce si**ŋ** as most English speakers do. Your mirror will be useful: /ŋ/ has the same tongue position as /g/, so start with /g/ and hold this position with the mouth wide open. Notice that the tip of the tongue is low in the mouth and that the back of the tongue is high. Hold this mouth position and at the same time start the humming note that you get with /m/ and /n/. Be sure that the mouth position does not change, and that the tip of the tongue does not rise at all. Continue the sound for three seconds, watching closely, then stop and start again. Keep your mouth wide open each time so that you can see that the tongue is in the right position. At the end of the sound just let it die away into silence with no suggestion of /g/. When you can do this easily, do the same thing with the teeth closer together in a more normal position, but be sure that the tip of the tongue stays in its low position. Now try the following words: make the final /ŋ/ long and let it die away into silence:

| sɪŋ sing | sæŋ sang | sɒŋ song | sʌŋ sung |
| rɪŋ ring | ræŋ rang | rɒŋ wrong | rʌŋ rung |

/ŋ/ does not occur at the beginning of words in English, but it does occur between vowels, where it is more difficult than in final position. The difficulty is to avoid putting in a /g/ after the /ŋ/, and pronouncing sɪŋgə instead of sɪŋə. If you do pronounce sɪŋgə it does not matter very much because some English speakers also do it; but most do not, so the /g/ should be avoided if possible. Go from the /ŋ/ to the following vowel very smoothly, with no jerk or bang. Try these examples, slowly at first, then more quickly:

Nasal consonants

sɪŋə	singer	lɒŋ əgəʊ	long ago
hæŋ ʌp	hang up	rɒŋ əgen	wrong again
sɪŋɪŋ	singing	hæŋɪŋ	hanging
brɪŋ ɪt	bring it	əmʌŋ ʌðəz	among others
lɒŋɪŋ	longing	bæŋɪŋ	banging

The most important thing is to keep /n/ and /ŋ/ separate and not to confuse them. Try the following pairs and be careful to keep the tongue-tip down for /n/:

sɪn	sin	sɪŋ	sing	sʌn	son	sʌŋ	sung
ræn	ran	ræŋ	rang	sɪnə	sinner	sɪŋə	singer
tʌnz	tons	tʌŋz	tongues				

In some words /g/ is normally pronounced after /ŋ/ before a following vowel, for example in æŋgə *anger*, fɪŋgə *finger*. A useful general rule is that if the word is formed from a *verb*, no /g/ is pronounced, as with sɪŋə, hæŋɪŋ, but if not, /g/ is pronounced, as in strɒŋgə, formed from the adjective strɒŋ *strong*, and æŋgə *anger*, which is not formed out of a shorter word. Notice the difference between lɒŋgə *longer* formed from the adjective *long*, and lɒŋɪŋ *longing* formed from the verb *long*. /g/ is never pronounced before a following consonant, for example: sɪŋz *sings*, bæŋd *banged*.

If you have the tendency to nasalize the vowel instead of pronouncing /ŋ/, mentioned on p. 50, you must be very careful to make a firm contact with the back of the tongue and force all the air to go through the nose.

Some of the commonest words containing /ŋ/ are: *anger, anxious, drink, finger, hungry, language, sink, thank, think, among(st), bring, during, evening, hang, -ing, long, morning, ring, sing, song, spring, string, strong, thing, wrong, young.*

3.4 Lateral consonant

One English consonant – /l/ – is formed laterally, that is, instead of the breath passing down the centre of the mouth, it passes round the sides of an obstruction set up in the centre. The position of the organs of speech for /l/ as in lɪv *live* is shown in Figure 23.

NOTICE
1 The soft palate is raised.
2 The tongue-tip (and the sides of the tongue-blade which cannot be

Consonants

seen in the diagram) are in firm contact with the alveolar ridge, obstructing the centre of the mouth.

3 The sides of the remainder of the tongue are not in contact with the sides of the palate, so air can pass between the sides of the tongue and the palate, round the central obstruction formed by the tip and blade of the tongue and so out of the mouth.

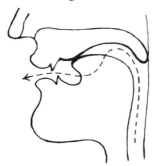

Fig. 23 /l/ *as in* lɪv

4 The sound is voiced and there is no friction (except when it is immediately after /p/ or /k/ – see pp. 40 and 45).

Most languages have a sound like English /l/, at least before vowels, and this can be used in such words as liːv *leave*, lɑːst *last*, lʊk *look*, fɒləʊ *follow*. Some languages, however (Japanese, for instance), do not have a satisfactory /l/ and such students must be very careful to make a firm contact of the tongue-tip and the sides of the blade with the alveolar ridge. If this is difficult for you try biting the tongue-tip firmly between top and bottom teeth; this will make a central obstruction and the air will be forced to pass over the sides of the tongue. In passing to the vowel the tongue-tip is removed from the alveolar ridge quite suddenly and the sound ends sharply; it may help to put in a very quick /d/-sound between the /l/ and the following vowel: lᵈiːv *leave*, etc.

Practise the following words, making the /l/ long and the central obstruction very firm to begin with:

liːf leaf	letə letter	lɒst lost	luːs loose
lɜːn learn	leɪt late	laɪk like	laʊd loud

When you are satisfied with /l/ in this position try these words, and be sure that the contact of the tongue-tip with the alveolar ridge is complete:

Lateral consonant

fiːlɪŋ feeling
feləʊ fellow
fuːlɪʃ foolish

hɒlədɪ holiday
bɪliːv believe
əlaʊ allow

Once you have a satisfactory /l/ before vowels you can use it in *all* positions without fear of being misunderstood; but many English people use different /l/-sounds before vowels and in other positions. For any /l/ the tongue-tip makes the usual firm contact, but before consonants and in final position the remainder of the tongue takes up a shape like that required for the vowel /ʊ/ or /ɔː/; before vowels the remainder of the tongue is placed as for the vowel /ɪ/. So the /l/ has a different 'colouring' in the two cases.

Make the tongue-tip contact firmly, and hold it whilst you say /ɪ/ as in sɪt – the two things must go on *at the same time*, not one after the other; this is the /l/ before vowels and it is known as the *clear* /l/. Now hold the contact firmly still and at the same time say the vowel /ʊ/, as in pʊt; this is the /l/ before consonants and in final positions, e.g. in fɪl *fill* and fɪld *filled*, and it is called the *dark* /l/. Many English speakers use only a clear /l/ in all positions, and many others use only a dark /l/ – which is why it is not very important for you to learn both – but most speakers of the kind of English described here do use both kinds of /l/. The words given for practice above would all contain clear /l/, because a vowel immediately follows (and this is true whether the vowel is in the same word or not, so both fiːlɪŋ and fiːl ɪt have clear /l/).

Whether or not you decide to use the English dark /l/ in the positions mentioned, some of you (e.g. Japanese, Cantonese) will need to be very careful with /l/ before consonants and in final position. The danger, and it is greater here than elsewhere, is that you do not make a firm contact of the tongue-tip with the alveolar ridge, the result being either some sort of vowel sound – fɪʊ, and fɪʊd for *fill* and *filled*, or some sort of /r/-sound – fɪr and fɪrd. The sound in English, whether it is dark or clear, must be a lateral, it must have the firm central obstruction and air escaping over the sides of the tongue. In the words below make the /l/ very carefully and be sure that the tongue-tip makes full and firm contact.

ɔːl	all	fʊl	full	tuːl	tool	sel	sell
bɪl	bill	fiːl	feel	teɪl	tail	maɪl	mile
aʊl	owl	ɔɪl	oil	kɔːld	called	pʊlz	pulls
fuːlz	fools	belt	belt	fiːld	field	kəʊld	cold
maɪlz	miles						

Consonants

/l/ is very often syllabic, like /n/ (p. 50), that is, it occurs in a position more usually occupied by a vowel; in words such as *parcel, level, puzzle, lethal, ruffle* most English people would pronounce pɑːsl̩, levl̩, pʌzl̩, liːθl̩, rʌfl̩/ with syllabic /l̩/, but it is also possible to pronounce pɑːsəl, etc., so do whichever is easiest.

After the stop consonants, however, as in *trouble, apple, bottle, middle, eagle*, it is less desirable to have a vowel between the stop and the /l̩/. Start with *apple* /æpl̩/: as soon as the lips are opened the /l̩/ is sounded immediately. Do the same with trʌbl̩. For tækl̩, hold the /k/ until the tip of the tongue is firmly in position for /l̩/, then release /k/. Do the same with iːgl̩. When /l/ follows /t/ and /d/, the stop sounds have a special release, which is dealt with on p. 72. If a vowel creeps in between any of the stop consonants and /l̩/, you will not be misunderstood, but this is not the usual English habit. Syllabic /l̩/ is usually dark /l/, but again the most important thing is to make an /l/-sound of some sort. Other examples of words containing syllabic /l̩/ are:

bjuːtəfl̩	beautiful	kæml̩	camel
ɔːfl̩	awful	kʌpl̩	couple
trævl̩	travel	baɪbl̩	Bible
wɪsl̩	whistle	tʃʌkl̩	chuckle
dæzl̩	dazzle	gɪgl̩	giggle
tʃænl̩	channel		

Some students (e.g. Cantonese) may have difficulty in distinguishing between /l/ and /n/ in initial position; this leads to pronouncing laɪf *life* as naɪf *knife* or nɒt *not* as lɒt *lot*, and must be avoided. Remember that /n/ is entirely nasal, all the air goes out of the nose; but /l/ is entirely oral, all the air goes out of the mouth. Try this: say a long /n/, and, whilst you are saying it, nip your nostrils so that the air cannot escape from the nose; this will interrupt the sound. Now say /l/ and do the same thing: if you are making /l/ correctly there will be no change at all; if there *is* a change it means that some air, or perhaps all the air, is passing through the nose, which is wrong for /l/. Do the same thing with a long /s/, and notice that nipping the nose makes no difference to the sound; then try /l/ again, until you are sure that you can always make it without any air going through the nose. It will be helpful to think of a slight /d/-sound in going from the /l/ to the following vowel, as mentioned above – l ᵈaɪf, l ᵈɒt, etc. When you are sure that your /n/ is entirely nasal and your /l/ entirely oral, practise distinguishing these pairs:

Lateral consonant

ləʊ low	nəʊ no	liːd lead	niːd need
laɪt light	naɪt night	leɪbə labour	neɪbə neighbour
let let	net net	lɪp lip	nɪp nip

Some of the commonest words containing /l/ are: *lady, land, language, last, late, laugh, lead, learn, leave, left, less, let, like, listen, little, live, long, lot, lack, lose, love, low, allow, along, almost, already, always, cold, colour, difficult, early, eleven, else, fault, -ly, help, o'clock, old, self, yellow, able, all, beautiful, fall, feel, fill, full, girl, meal, mile, parcel, people, possible, real, school, shall, still, table, tell, until, well.*

3.5 Gliding consonants

There are three consonants which consist of a quick, smooth, non-friction glide towards a following vowel sound, the consonants /j, w, r/.

/j/

This consonant is a quick glide from the position of the vowel /iː/ or /ɪ/ to any other vowel. We usually transcribe the word *yes* as jes, but we might easily transcribe it iːes or ɪes, on the understanding that the /iː/ or /ɪ/ is very short and that we move smoothly and quickly to the following /e/. Try the following words in that way, and be sure that there is no friction in the /j/-glide:

jɑːd yard	jet yet
jɒt yacht	juː you
jɔː your	

The same is true in the following words where /j/ is not initial; make a quick, weak /iː/-sound before the following vowel:

| bjuːtɪ beauty | djuː due | fjuː few | vjuː view |
| vælju: value | njuː new | mjuːzɪk music | |

When /j/ follows /p, t, k/ it loses the voice which it usually has, and is made voiceless; this causes some friction to be heard, and it is important to do this because otherwise the stop consonants may be heard as /b, d, g/, and the word *tune* tjuːn confused with *dune* djuːn. Try the following words, making /j/ in the same way as before *except* that you let breath take the place of voice:

57

Consonants

tjuːzdɪ Tuesday	kəmpjuːtə computer
tjuːn tune	kjuː queue
pjʊə pure	əkjuːz accuse

Some English people use /tʃ/ instead of /tj/ and /dʒ/ instead of /dj/, pronouncing tʃuːzdɪ instead of tjuːzdɪ *Tuesday*, and dʒuː instead of djuː *due*, but this is not generally accepted and should be avoided.

Most American speakers do not use /j/ in words where it would follow /t, d, n, l, s, θ/, pronouncing tuːn *tune*, duː *due*, nuː *new*, æbsəluːt *absolute*, suːt *suit*, and ɪnθuːzɪæzəm *enthusiasm*. R.P. speakers always use /j/ after /t, d, n/ in such words, but some do not use it after /l, s, θ/. If your model is American, do not pronounce /j/ after these consonants; if not, it is probably better to use /j/ after all of them. /j/ does not occur in final position.

Some of the commonest words containing /j/ are: *yard, year, yellow, yes, yesterday, yet, you, young, your, use, usual, useful, Europe, amuse, beautiful, cure, during, duty, educate, excuse, failure, few, huge, January, knew, music, new, suit, Tuesday, value.*

/w/

This consonant consists of a quick glide from the vowel /uː/ or /ʊ/ to whatever vowel follows. It is much more difficult than /j/ because many languages do not have an independent /w/. But it is not difficult to learn to say. Start with /uː/ or /ʊ/ and follow this immediately by the vowel /ɔː/ – this is the word wɔː *war*. The /w/ part must be short and weak, as with /j/, but the lips must be rounded quite firmly – even English people move their lips noticeably for /w/!

Try these words in the same way, beginning each with a very short weak /uː/ or /ʊ/ with the lips well rounded:

wɒtʃ watch	wɪn win	weə where
wet wet	wiː we	wʊd wood
waɪt white	weɪt wait	wʊl wool

When /w/ follows a consonant it is made in the same way; but the lips are rounded ready for /w/ before the previous consonant is finished. So in swiːt *sweet* the lips gradually become rounded during the /s/, and when it ends they are firmly rounded ready for /w/. This is true for all the following words; try them:

swiːt sweet	swɪm swim	swet sweat
sweə swear	dwelɪŋ dwelling	

Gliding consonants

You must remember too that when /w/ immediately follows /t/ or /k/ the glide is not voiced, though the lips are again rounded during the stop consonant. Try the following words, round the lips early, and blow out breath through them:

twaɪs twice	twentɪ twenty	twelv twelve	twɪn twin
kwaɪt quite	kwɪk quick	kwaɪət quiet	kwiːn queen

/w/ is particularly difficult for those (like Germans, Dutch, many Indians) who have a sound like English /v/ but none like /w/. These speakers tend to replace /w/ by /v/ and say vel instead of wel *well*. This must be avoided and you can do this by concentrating on pairs like those below. For the /v/ words, keep the lips flat and use the upper teeth to make some friction; for the /w/ words there is no friction and the lips are well rounded.

vɜːs verse	wɜːs worse	vaɪn vine	waɪn wine
viːl veal	wiːl wheel	vaɪl vile	waɪl while
veərɪ vary	weərɪ wary	veɪl veil	weɪl wail

When you are able to make /w/ easily, be careful not to use it instead of /v/. It is just as bad to say werɪ for *very* as to say vel for *well*.

Now try the following similar pairs with the /w/ and the /v/ between vowels, taking care to make a good difference:

rɪwɔːd reward	rɪviːl reveal
fɔːwəd forward	hɒvəd hovered
əweɪ away	əveɪl avail
haɪweɪ highway	daɪvə diver

Words such as *which, when, where, why* (but not *who*) are pronounced with simple /w/ in R.P.: wɪtʃ, wen, weə, waɪ, etc. In some other kinds of English (e.g. American, Scottish, Irish) they begin with /hw/. If your model is one of these, you can begin these words with a completely voiceless /w/ instead of the voiced one.

/w/ does not occur in final position.

Some of the commonest words containing /w/ are: *one, wait, walk, want, warm, wash, watch, water, way, we, week, well, wet, what, when, why, will, wish, with, woman, word, work, always, away, between, quarter, question, quick, quite, sweet, swim, twelve, twenty, twice.*

/r/

This is the third of the gliding consonants, but it does not resemble one

Consonants

of the English vowels as /j/ and /w/ do. The position of the speech organs for /r/ is shown in Figure 24.

NOTICE
1 The tongue has a curved shape with the tip pointing towards the hard palate at the back of the alveolar ridge, the front low and the back rather high.
2 The tongue-tip is not close enough to the palate to cause friction.
3 The lips are rather rounded, especially when /r/ is at the beginning of words.
4 The soft palate is raised; and voiced air flows quietly between the tongue-tip and palate with no friction.

Foreign learners often replace this sound by the sound which is represented by the letter *r* in their own language. Sometimes they use a *rolled* sound in which the tip of the tongue taps very quickly several times against the alveolar ridge (Italian, Arabic, Russian) or the uvula taps against the back of the tongue in a similar way (Dutch, French, German). Sometimes they use a friction sound with the back of the tongue close to the soft palate and uvula (Danish, French, German). Such sounds are perfectly well understood by English people, but of course they sound foreign.

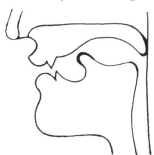

Fig. 24 /r/

Try approaching the English sound from a /w/. Get the speech organs ready for /w/ (remember that this is a short /ʊ/-or /uː/-sound), and then curl the tip of the tongue back until it is pointing at the hard palate, quite a long way behind the alveolar ridge. Now change smoothly and without friction to the following vowel, as in red *red*. Be careful, if you have an /r/-sound in your language, not to make it at the same time as the English sound: try to think of English /r/ as a new

Gliding consonants

sound altogether. Try these words and be sure that the tongue-tip is well back in the mouth at the beginning of the glide:

| riːd read | red red | rʌn run | rɔː raw |
| ruːd rude | reɪs race | raʊnd round | reə rare |

Between vowels the sound is the same except that the lips are not rounded. Try the following, and concentrate on getting the tongue-tip up and back, then smoothly down and forward again:

| verɪ very | mærɪ marry | bɒrəʊ borrow | hʌrɪ hurry |
| əraɪv arrive | kərekt correct | əraʊnd around | ərest arrest |

In R.P. /r/ only occurs before vowels, never before consonants, so words like *learn, sort, farm* do not contain /r/ (lɜːn, sɔːt, fɑːm). Other varieties of English pronounce /r/ in these words (e.g. American, Irish, Scottish), so if your model is one of these, you will pronounce /r/ before consonants; if it is R.P. you will not. At the end of words R.P. has /r/ only if the immediately following word begins with a vowel; so the word *never*, if it occurs before a pause or before a word beginning with a consonant (as in *never better*), is pronounced nevə with no /r/ in R.P. But in *never again* where it is immediately followed by a vowel /r/ is pronounced, nevər əgen. This is called the *linking* /r/; some R.P. speakers do not use it (and say nevə əgen), so you may do this if you find it easier, but most people do use it.

Try these phrases, either with or without the /r/:

| betər ɒf   better off | hɪər ɪt ɪz   here it is |
| fɔːr ɔː faɪv   four or five | pʊər əʊld tɒm   poor old Tom |

It is quite usual to hear this linking /r/ following the vowel /ə/ even when there is no letter *r* in the spelling, as in *Africa and Asia* æfrɪkər ən eɪʃə, *Linda and Ann* lɪndər ən æn. Some English speakers dislike this so-called 'intrusive /r/', so it is perhaps best for you not to use it. You may also hear it after the vowel /ɔː/ as in *I saw a man* aɪ sɔːr ə mæn, but here very many English speakers disapprove of it, and you should not use it.

There is danger of confusing /r/ with /l/ (e.g. for Cantonese and Japanese speakers) and also with /n/ (Cantonese). Remember that for /n/ and /l/ there is a very firm contact of the tongue-tip with the alveolar ridge (/n/ being nasal, and /l/ oral, see p. 56), but for /r/ the tongue-tip does not touch the palate at all – it is purely a gliding sound, with no sudden change. Try the following, and concentrate on the very firm contact for /l/ and /n/, and a smooth glide (like /w/) for /r/:

Consonants

laɪt light	naɪt night	raɪt right
ləʊ low	nəʊ no	rəʊ row
liːd lead	niːd need	riːd read
lɒk lock	nɒk knock	rɒk rock

The difficulty is greatest between vowels, so be most careful with the following:

belɪ belly	benɪ Bennie	berɪ berry
kɔːl əs call us	kɔːnəz corners	kɔːrəs chorus
spɪl ɪt spill it	spɪn ɪt spin it	spɪrɪt spirit
telə teller	tenə tenor	terə terror

After /p, t, k/ there is no voice in /r/. The tongue position is the same, but pure breath is pushed through the space between the tongue-tip and the hard palate, causing friction. Try with /p/ first; close the lips for /p/, then put the tongue in position for /r/, and, as the lips open for /p/, push breath strongly over the tongue-tip so that you can hear friction before the following vowel:

preɪ pray	praʊd proud
præm pram	kəmpres compress
əpruːv approve	dɪpraɪv deprive

Now try /kr/: take up the position for /k/; then put the tongue-tip in position for /r/ and, when the /k/ is released, push breath through to cause friction:

kriːm cream	kruəl cruel
kræk crack	ɪŋkriːs increase
rɪkruːt recruit	dɪkriːs decrease

When /t/ occurs before /r/, the tongue-tip for /t/ is placed *behind* the alveolar ridge, on the front of the hard palate, so that when it is removed the tongue is immediately in position for the friction of /r/. Be sure that in the following words the tongue-tip is a good deal further back than usual for /t/:

triː tree	traɪ try	truː true	trʌst trust
ətrækt attract	rɪtriːt retreat	ɪntruːd intrude	

This /tr/ combination may be confused with /tʃ/; notice that the friction of the voiceless /r/ is *lower* in pitch than that of /ʃ/. Try the

Gliding consonants

following pairs and be careful to put the tongue-tip in the correct /r/ position for /tr/:

| tru: true | tʃu: chew | trɪp trip | tʃɪp chip |
| treɪn train | tʃeɪn chain | træp trap | tʃæp chap |

In the combination /dr/ too the tip of the tongue is further back than usual for /d/ and there is friction as the voiced air passes over the tongue-tip for the /r/. Try these words:

| dri:m dream | draɪ dry | dres dress | drɒp drop |
| drɔ: draw | dru:p droop | ədres address | |

And the following pairs must be distinguished in the same way as /tr/ and /tʃ/:

| dreɪn drain | dʒeɪn Jane | drɔ: draw | dʒɔ: jaw |
| dru: drew | dʒu: Jew | drʌŋk drunk | dʒʌŋk junk |

Some of the commonest words containing /r/ are: *rain, rather, reach, read, ready, real, red, remember, rest, right, road, roof, room, round, rule, run, write, wrong, agree, already, arrange, borrow, bread, bring, cross, direct, dress, drink, every, foreign, from, great, interest, marry, pretty, price, serious, sorry, story, terrible, true, try, very, worry.*

3.6 Exercises

1 Study each section carefully and decide what your difficulties are. Which of these difficulties are *phoneme* difficulties (e.g. confusing /s/ and /θ/ or /t/ and /d/), and which are purely *sound* difficulties (e.g. pronouncing /t/ with the tongue-tip on the teeth instead of on the alveolar ridge)? Which difficulties will you concentrate on?
2 During the time which you give to listening to English, concentrate for a short time on listening to *one* of your difficulties (perhaps the difference between /s/ and /θ/, or the sound of /h/). When you have really *heard* the sound(s), go back to the lists of words in the different sections and try to make the sound exactly the same as you heard. Use a tape-recorder to help you, if you can.
3 Take any passage of English and mark any one of your difficulties all the way through (e.g. underline every *l* or *r* or both). Then read the passage aloud, and try to say particular sounds perfectly. Don't worry about the others at that moment. Gradually do this for *all* your difficulties.
4 Do a little practice *each day* if you possibly can.

4 Consonant sequences

In chapter 3 we saw how single consonants are made, and sometimes how a sequence of two consonants should be said (e.g. /pr, kr, tr/ p. 62), but there are many other cases where two or three or four or even more consonants follow one after the other. Some examples are: skiːm *scheme*, kriːm *cream*, skriːm *scream*, neks *necks*, nekst *next*, teksts *texts*.

Some languages (e.g. Russian, German) have many consonant sequences, and speakers of these languages will not have any difficulty in pronouncing most of the English ones. But other languages do not have sequences of consonants at all, or only very few and very short ones (e.g. Mandarin, Cantonese, Vietnamese, Swahili, Yoruba, Tamil), and speakers of these languages (in which two consonants are usually separated by a vowel) may have difficulty in stringing together two, three or four consonants with no vowel between them. This chapter is to help you, if you have this kind of difficulty.

4.1 Initial sequences

At the beginning of English words there may be either two or three consonants in sequence.

Sequences of two consonants initially

These are of two main kinds:
1 /s/ followed by one of /p, t, k, f, m, n, l, w, j/, e.g. in *spy, stay, sky, sphere, small, snow, sleep, swear, suit*.
2 One of /p, t, k, b, d, g, f, θ, ʃ, v, m, n, h/ followed by one of /l, r, w, j/. Not all of these sequences are found (e.g. /pw, dl/ do not occur). The full list is:

/p/	followed by	/l, r, j/	play, pray, pure
/t/		/r, w, j/	try, twice, tune
/k/		/l, r, w, j/	climb, cry, quite, cure

Initial sequences

/b/	/l, r, j/	blow, bread, beauty
/d/	/r, w, j/	dress, dwell (rare), duty
/g/	/l, r/	glass, green
/f/	/l, r, j/	fly, from, few
/θ/	/r, w/	throw, thwart (rare)
/ʃ/	/r/	shriek
/v/	/j/	view
/m/	/j/	music
/n/	/j/	new
/h/	/j/	huge

Start with /sp/: say a long /s/, then gradually close the lips for /p/ until they stop the /s-/sound. Keep the /s/ going right up to the moment *after* the lips are closed, and you will not put a vowel between the two consonants. Be careful to start with a long /s/ and do not put a vowel before it. Do this many times until you are sure that there is no vowel sound either before the /s/ or after it. Now add the vowel in words such as:

spaɪ spy	spɜː spur	spɪə spear	speə spare

Do not say əspaɪ or səpaɪ. Start with /s/ and halt it by closing the lips.

/st/ and /sk/ are begun by making a long /s/ and halting it by raising the tongue-tip (for /st/) or tongue-back (for /sk/) to cut off the friction. Try:

steɪ stay	staː star	stɔː store	stɪə steer
skaɪ sky	skaː scar	skɔː score	skeə scare

Do not say əsteɪ or səteɪ, etc.

In /sf/ (which is rare) the long /s/ is ended by the lower lip moving up to the upper teeth for /f/:

sfɪə sphere	sferɪkəl spherical

In /sm/, the /s/ is continued until the lips meet for /m/, and in /sn, sl/, until the tongue-tip touches the alveolar ridge. (Those of you who have trouble with /l/ and /r/ must be careful not to pronounce sriːp for sliːp *sleep* (see p. 61).)

smaɪl smile	sməʊk smoke	smel smell	smɪə smear
snəʊ snow	snɔː snore	sneɪk snake	snæk snack
sləʊ slow	slaɪ sly	slɪp slip	slæk slack

Consonant sequences

In /sw/ the lips become rounded during the /s/ (be careful not to pronounce /sv/) and in /sj/ the /iː/, which is the beginning of the /j/-glide, is reached during the /s/, so that in both cases the glide starts as soon as /s/ ends. Try:

| swiːt sweet | sweɪ sway | swɒn swan | swuːp swoop |
| sjuːt suit | sjuː sue | əsjuːm assume | pəsjuː pursue |

In the second group of sequences, the second consonant is most often formed whilst the first one is being pronounced. For example, in /pr/ or /pl/ the tongue is placed in the exact position for /r/ or /l/ whilst the lips are still closed for the /p/, so that as soon as they are open the /r/ or /l/ is heard. In the following examples start with a long first consonant, and during it place the tongue (and for /w/ the lips) in position for the second consonant; then, and only then, release the first consonant:

pleɪ play	preɪ pray	pjʊə pure	traɪ try
twaɪs twice	tjuːn tune	klaɪm climb	kraɪ cry
kwaɪt quite	kjʊə cure	bləʊ blow	bred bread
bjuːtɪ beauty	dres dress	dwel dwell	djuːtɪ duty
glɑːs glass	griːn green	flaɪ fly	frɒm from
fjuː few	vjuː view	mjuːzɪk music	njuː new

In /θr/ and /ʃr/ the second consonant cannot be prepared during the first. Be sure first of all that you can pronounce each one separately; say one, then the other, several times. Then smoothly and continuously make the tongue glide from one to the other so that there is no sudden change between them; try the following, very slowly at first, then gradually quicker:

| θrəʊ throw | θriː three | θred thread | θruː threw |
| ʃriːk shriek | ʃred shred | ʃrɪl shrill | ʃruːd shrewd |

Sequences of three consonants initially

These are /spr, str, skr, spj, stj, skj, spl, skw/ and are a combination of the /sp/ type of sequence and the /pr/ type. The /s/ at the beginning is cut off by the following stop, and during the stop the following consonant is fully prepared. Try the following examples very slowly at first; cut off the /s/ by the tongue or lips and, whilst holding this stop, get the third consonant ready, then release the stop straight into the third consonant:

Initial sequences

spred	spread	stjuːpɪd	stupid
streɪt	straight	skjʊə	skewer
skruː	screw	splendɪd	splendid
spjʊərɪəs	spurious	skweə	square

The sequence /spj/ is rare.

4.2 Final sequences

Sequences of consonants at the ends of words are more varied than at the beginning mainly because /s/ or /z/ have to be added to most nouns to give their plural forms, as in kæts *cats*, dɒgz *dogs*, fækts *facts*, fiːldz *fields*, etc., and /t/ or /d/ have to be added to most verbs to form their past tense, as in wɪʃt *wished*, reɪzd *raised*, rɪskt *risked*, plʌndʒd *plunged*, etc. Also /θ/ is used to form nouns like streŋθ *strength* and bredθ *breadth* and numerals like fɪfθ *fifth* (and all these can have plurals – streŋθs, bredθs, fɪfθs!).

Stop+stop

When one stop consonant is immediately followed by another, as in kept *kept* and ækt *act*, the closure of the speech organs for the second consonant is made whilst the closure for the first consonant is still in position. In the sequence /pt/ this is what happens: the lips are closed

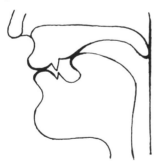

Fig. 25 Double closure in /pt/

for /p/ and air is compressed as usual by pressure from the lungs; then, with the lips still closed, the tongue-tip is placed on the alveolar ridge ready for /t/, so that there are two closures, see Figure 25. Then, and only then, the lips are opened, but there is no explosion of air because the tongue closure prevents the compressed air from bursting out of the mouth; finally, the tongue-tip leaves the alveolar ridge and air explodes out of the mouth. So there is only one explosion for the two stops; the first stop is incomplete.

Figure 26 shows a similar position for the sequence /kt/. First the back of the tongue makes the closure for /k/, then the tip of the tongue makes the closure for /t/, then the back of the tongue is lowered without causing an explosion, and finally the tongue-tip is lowered and air explodes out.

Start with **kept**. First say **kep** and hold the air back with the lips, don't open them. Now put the tongue-tip in position for /t/ (lips still closed). Now open the lips and be sure that no air comes out, and then lower the tongue-tip and allow the air out. Do this several times and be sure that the lips are firmly closed (we do not say **ket**) and that the tongue-tip is ready to hold back the breath before you open the lips. Then do the same with **ækt**, and be sure that although /k/ is properly formed, its ending is, as it were swallowed, so that there is no explosion until the /t/ is released.

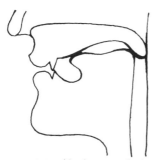

Fig. 26 Double closure in /kt/

Now do exactly the same for /bd/ as in **rɒbd** *robbed* and /gd/ as in **drægd** *dragged*. Again there is only one explosion, this time a gentle one for the /d/. If you do make two explosions it will not cause any misunderstanding, but it will sound un-English. What is important is to be sure that the first consonant is properly formed before you take up the position for the second. If you say **rɒd** instead of **rɒbd** or **dræd** instead of **drægd**, you will be misunderstood.

This 'missing explosion' happens whenever one stop consonant (except /tʃ/ and /dʒ/) is followed immediately by another (including /tʃ/ and /dʒ/), not only at the end of words but also in the middle of words, as in **æktə** *actor*, or between words, as in **red kəʊt** *red coat*. Here are some examples for practice:

Final sequences

slept	slept	fækt	fact
rʌbd	rubbed	drʌgd	drugged
tɒp dɒg	top dog	ʃɒp gɜːl	shop girl
raɪp təmɑːtəʊ	ripe tomato	eɪtpəns	eightpence
greɪt keə	great care	hɒt bɑːθ	hot bath
kwaɪt gʊd	quite good	θɪk piːs	thick piece
blækbɜːd	blackbird	blæk dɒg	black dog
klʌb taɪ	club tie	sʌbkɒnʃəs	subconscious
bɒb gʊdwɪn	Bob Goodwin	red pɜːs	red purse
bæd kəʊld	bad cold	gʊdbaɪ	goodbye
aɪd gəʊ	I'd go	bægpaɪps	bagpipes
pɪgteɪl	pigtail	bɪg bɔɪ	big boy
lektʃə	lecture	ɒbdʒɪkt	object (n.)
bɪg dʒəʊk	big joke	tʃiːp tʃiːz	cheap cheese

When /p/ is followed by /p/, or /t/ by /t/, and so on, there is again only one explosion, but the closure is held for double the usual time. Examples:

slɪp pɑːst	slip past	wɒt taɪm	what time?
lʊk keəfəlɪ	look carefully	bɒb beɪts	Bob Bates
mæd dɒg	mad dog	bɪg gɜːl	big girl

For /tʃ/ and /dʒ/ the friction part of the sound is never missing, so in wɪtʃ tʃeə *which chair?* and lɑːdʒ dʒʌg *large jug* the /tʃ/ and /dʒ/ are complete in both places.

When one of the strong/weak pair /p, b/ or /t, d/ or /k, g/ is followed by the other, for example in wɒt deɪ *what day* or bɪg keɪk *big cake*, there is only one explosion, but the closure is held for double the usual time and the strength changes during this time. Other examples are:

hɪp bəʊn	hip bone
bed taɪm	bed-time
blæk gəʊt	black goat

If three stop consonants come together, as in strɪkt peərənt *strict parent*, there is still only one explosion, that of the third consonant. What usually happens is that the first consonant is formed and held for longer than usual, the second consonant disappears altogether, and the third is formed and exploded normally. We might write *strict parent* as strɪkː peərənt, where /kː/ represents an unexploded /k/ held for longer than usual. Other examples are:

Consonant sequences

aɪ slept bædlɪ	I slept badly
hiː lægd bɪhaɪnd	he lagged behind
kəlәkt penɪz	collect pennies
ðeɪ rɒbd kɑːz	they robbed cars

/pt/ and /kt/ can be followed immediately by /s/ in words like əksepts *accepts* and fækts *facts*. In these sequences /p/ and /k/ are not exploded but the /t/ explodes straight into the /s/. Be sure to form the first stop firmly. Other examples are:

ɪntərʌpts	interrupts	ədɒpts	adopts
kɒntækts	contacts	prətekts	protects
rɪækts	reacts		

Stop+nasal

When /t/ or /d/ are followed by a syllabic /n̩/, as in bʌtn̩ *button* and gɑːdn̩ *garden*, the explosion of the stop takes place through the nose. This *nasal explosion* happens in this way: the vocal organs form /t/ or /d/ in the usual way, with the soft palate raised to shut off the nasal cavity and the tongue-tip on the alveolar ridge, but instead of taking the tongue-tip away from the alveolar ridge to give the explosion we leave it in the same position and lower the soft palate, so that the breath explodes out of the nose rather than out of the mouth. Figure 27 shows

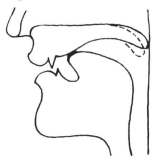

Fig. 27 Nasal explosion in /tn/

that this is the simplest way of passing from /t/ or /d/ to /n/, since the tongue position is the same for all three consonants and the only difference is in the raised or lowered position of the soft palate.

Make a /t/-sound and hold the breath in the mouth, don't let it out; then send all the breath out sharply through the nose (just as in the

Final sequences

exercise described on p. 16) whilst still holding the tongue-tip firmly against the alveolar ridge. Do this several times without allowing the tongue-tip to move at all and feel the air bursting out behind the soft palate. Now start the voice vibrating for /n/ as the soft palate lowers and again do this several times without moving the tongue-tip. Now do the same thing for /dn/, with the voice vibrating through both /d/ and /n/ but the tongue-tip firmly on the alveolar ridge all the time. The effect in both /tn/ and /dn/ is to make the explosion of the stop much less clear than when it bursts out of the mouth; if you do make the explosion by taking the tongue-tip away from the alveolar ridge or if you put the vowel /ə/ between the /t/ or /d/ and the /n/ it will sound rather strange to English ears, but you will not be misunderstood. Try these other similar words:

rɪtn̩	written	brɪtn̩	Britain
hɪdn̩	hidden	bɜːdn̩	burden
sɜːtn̩	certain	fraɪtn̩	frighten
pɑːdn̩	pardon	wʊdn̩	wooden

Both /tn̩/ and /dn̩/ may be followed by /s/ or /z/ or /t/ or /d/, in words like ɪmpɔːtn̩s *importance*, kɜːtn̩z *curtains*, ɪmpɔːtn̩t *important* and fraɪtn̩d *frightened*. When the third consonant is /t/ or /d/ the tongue does not move at all – the soft palate is simply raised again to make the stop complete. For /s/ or /z/ the tongue-tip is lowered very slightly from the alveolar ridge to make the necessary friction. Try the following:

pɪtn̩s	pittance	ɔːtn̩t	oughtn't
pɑːdn̩d	pardoned	rɪdn̩s	riddance
wʊdn̩t	wouldn't	bʌtn̩z	buttons
gɑːdn̩z	gardens	ʃɔːtn̩d	shortened

In words where the /n/ is not syllabic, such as braɪtnɪs *brightness* and gʊdnɪs *goodness*, the explosion is also nasal, and this is also true when the stop is found at the end of one word and the /n/ at the beginning of the next, as in leɪt naɪt *late night* and bæd njuːz *bad news*. Try the following examples, and be sure that the tongue-tip stays firmly on the alveolar ridge through both /t/ and /n/:

waɪtnɪs	whiteness	wɪtnɪs	witness
sædnɪs	sadness	kɪdnɪ	kidney
ət naɪt	at night	wɒt nekst	what next?
gʊd naɪt	good night	red nəʊz	red nose

Consonant sequences

pɑːtnə	partner	laʊdnɪs	loudness
stɑːt naʊ	start now	bred naɪf	bread knife

Nasal explosion also happens when /m/ follows /t/ or /d/: the soft palate is lowered whilst the tongue-tip is firmly on the alveolar ridge and the lips are then quickly closed for /m/. It is usually more difficult in this case to keep the tongue-tip position until after the breath has exploded through the nose, so you must take care to hold it there. Try the following:

ʌtməʊst	utmost	ætməsfɪə	atmosphere
ɪksaɪtmənt	excitement	ədmaɪə	admire
ədmɪt	admit	ɒdmənt	oddment
ə bɪt mɔː	a bit more	waɪt maɪs	white mice
eɪt men	eight men	sæd mjuːzɪk	sad music
ə gʊd menɪ	a good many	brɔːd maɪndɪd	broad-minded

When you can do this well, you will not find much difficulty with /p, b, k, g/ followed by /m/ or /n/, in words like heɪpnɪ *halfpenny* or sɪknɪs *sickness*, or in phrases like teɪk maɪn *take mine* or bɪg mæn *big man*, where the explosion is also nasal. The secret is to hold the stop until the breath has exploded through the nose and only then to change the tongue or lip position for the nasal (if any change is needed). Try the following:

raɪpnɪs	ripeness	tɒpməʊst	topmost
əknɒlɪdʒ	acknowledge	frægmənt	fragment
stɒp naʊ	stop now	help miː	help me
dɑːk naɪt	dark night	teɪk maɪn	take mine
klʌb nəʊtɪs	club notice	bɪg nəʊz	big nose
bɪg maʊθ	big mouth		

/t/ or /d/ + /l/

/t/ and /d/ are made with the tongue-tip on the alveolar ridge and the sides of the tongue firmly touching the sides of the palate; /l/ is made with the tongue-tip touching the alveolar ridge, but the sides of the tongue away from the sides of the palate so that the breath passes out laterally. The simplest way to go from /t/ or /d/ to /l/ is to leave the tongue-tip on the alveolar ridge and only lower the sides, and that is what we do. It is called *lateral explosion*.

Make the closure for /d/ and hold it; then immediately change to /l/

Final sequences

but be sure that the tongue-tip does not leave the alveolar ridge even for a moment. If you find this difficult try *biting* the tip of your tongue so that it cannot move and then changing to /l/, until you have got the feeling of the breath exploding over the lowered sides of the tongue; then try it with the tongue-tip in its normal position. Do this several times, and then try the same action for /tl/. When you are satisfied that the tongue-tip does not move, try the following:

mɪdl̩ middle   mʌdl̩ muddle
bætl̩ battle   lɪtl̩ little

The plural ending /z/ and the past tense ending /d/ can be added to /tl̩/ and /dl̩/. For /tl̩d/ and /dl̩d/, as in bɒtl̩d *bottled* and mʌdl̩d *muddled*, the tongue-tip does not move at all; the sides are lowered for /l/ and raised again for /d/. For /tl̩z/ and /dl̩z/, as in bɒtl̩z *bottles* and niːdl̩z *needles*, the tongue-tip is lowered slightly from the alveolar ridge to give the necessary friction at the same time as the sides are raised to touch the sides of the palate, which they must do for /z/. Try the following:

hʌdl̩d huddled   kɜːdl̩d curdled
mɒdl̩z models   pedl̩z pedals
taɪtl̩d titled   mɒtl̩d mottled
taɪtl̩z titles   bætl̩z battles

In all the examples above /l/ is syllabic (see p. 56), but in words such as sædlɪ *sadly* and θɔːtlɪs *thoughtless* and in phrases like bæd laɪt *bad light* and streɪt laɪn *straight line*, where the /l/ is not syllabic, the explosion takes place in the same way, with the tongue-tip kept firmly on the alveolar ridge. Try the following:

bædlɪ badly   niːdlɪs needless
hɑːtlɪs heartless   leɪtlɪ lately
ət lɑːst at last   ʃɔːt laɪf short life
red laɪt red light   gʊd lʌk good luck

Notice, by the way, that in changing from /n/ to /l/ in words like tʃænl̩ *channel* and mænlɪ *manly* and in phrases like griːn liːf *green leaf*, the tongue-tip also stays on the alveolar ridge whilst the sides of the tongue are lowered. Try the following:

pænl̩ panel   fɪnlənd Finland
tʌnl̩ tunnel   tɜːn left turn left
ʌnles unless   wʌn les one less

Consonant sequences

Try also the following:

pæn|z panels   tʌn|z tunnels
tʃæn|d channeled   tʌn|d tunneled

Consonant +/s, z, t, d/

Because of the way in which regular plurals are formed in English there are very many sequences of a consonant followed by /s/ or /z/, for example lɪps *lips*, bɜːdz *birds*, sneɪks *snakes*, henz *hens*. And because of the way in which regular past tenses are formed there are also very many sequences of a consonant followed by /t/ or /d/, for example, kɪst *kissed*, lʌvd *loved*, lɑːft *laughed*, juːzd *used*.

When you make these sequences, be sure always to form the first consonant firmly and then to put the tongue into position for the /s/ or /z/ or the /t/ or /d/ whilst you are still continuing the first consonant. For example, in kʌps *cups* the lips are closed firmly for /p/ and then behind them the tongue-tip is placed in position for /s/, so that when the lips are opened for the release of /p/ the /s/ is heard immediately. The sounds flow into each other; there must never be an interval or hesitation or vowel between them. Try the following:

kʌps	cups	kæts	cats
wiːks	weeks	lɑːfs	laughs
dʒɒbz	jobs	gʊdz	goods
dæmz	dams	tɜːnz	turns
egz	eggs	draɪvz	drives
sɒŋz	songs	welz	wells
lɑːft	laughed	mɪst	missed
wɒʃt	washed	wɒtʃt	watched
pruːvd	proved	briːðd	breathed
siːmd	seemed	əʊnd	owned
geɪzd	gazed	dʒʌdʒd	judged
bæŋd	banged	fɪld	filled

Seven of these sequences /ps, ks, nz, ft, st, nd, ld/ occur in words which are not plurals or past forms; these sequences may then have yet another consonant added to them to form plurals and past forms, for example fɪkst *fixed* or gests *guests*. For these the tongue-tip must be either raised to make contact with the alveolar ridge to make /t/ or /d/, or it must be lowered slightly from the alveolar ridge to make the friction of /s/ or /z/. Be sure that the first two consonants are firmly but smoothly formed before adding the third. Try the following:

Final sequences

læpst	lapsed	brɒnzd	bronzed
tækst	taxed	lɪfts	lifts
rests	rests	fiːldz	fields
bendz	bends		

The sequence /ksts/ occurs in the word **teksts** *texts;* the last /s/ is again added by lowering the tongue slightly from the /t/ position to give the /s/ friction.

Also, the more common word **sɪksθ** *sixth* has /θ/ added to /ks/. This needs a smooth but definite movement of the tongue-tip from its position close to the alveolar ridge to a position close to the upper teeth; this will not be difficult if you have mastered the exercises on pp. 33–4.

Consonant + /θ/

The consonants /t, d, n, l/ are followed by /θ/ in the words **eɪtθ** *eighth*, **bredθ** *breadth*, **tenθ** *tenth* and **helθ** *health*. Normally /t, d, n/ and /l/ are made with the tongue-tip on the alveolar ridge, but when followed by /θ/ they are made with the tongue-tip touching the back of the upper teeth. It is then pulled away slightly to give the dental friction of /θ/.

In the words **fɪfθ** *fifth* and **leŋθ** *length* the tongue-tip is placed in position for /θ/ during the previous consonant, so that again there is no gap between them. There are only a few other words like these – **wɪdθ** *width*, **hʌndrədθ** *hundredth*, **naɪnθ** *ninth*, **θɜːtiːnθ** *thirteenth*, etc., **welθ** *wealth*, **streŋθ** *strength*. Practise these and those given above until you can go smoothly from the first consonant to the /θ/.

All of these words may then have a plural /s/ added, giving **eɪtθs** *eighths*, **bredθs** *breadths*, etc. The added /s/ should not be difficult if you have mastered the exercises on p. 34. The secret is a smooth but definite movement of the tongue-tip from the dental position of /θ/ to the alveolar position of /s/. Practise the plurals of all the words given above.

Notice also the word **twelfθ** *twelfth*, where /fθ/ has /l/ before it. Make sure that the /l/ is properly formed, and then during the /l/ raise the lower lip up to the upper teeth for /f/ and then go on to /θ/. This word also has the plural form **twelfθs**. Once again move the tongue-tip smoothly but firmly from the /θ/ to the /s/ position.

/l/ + consonant

Various consonants may follow /l/; we have already dealt with /lz/, /lθ/ and /ld/ on p. 74 and the remainder are not very difficult if you have

Consonant sequences

mastered /l/ by itself. Before any consonant the /l/ will be dark (see p. 55) and the following consonant is formed whilst the /l/ is being pronounced. Try the following:

help help	fɒlt fault	mɪlk milk	ʃelf shelf
elʃ else	welʃ Welsh	ʃelv shelve	bʌldʒ bulge
fɪlm film			

Plural and past forms lengthen some of these sequences as before. Try:

helps helps	helpt helped	belts belts	mɪlks milks
mɪlkt milked	ʃelvz shelves	bʌldʒd bulged	fɪlmz films
fɪlmd filmed			

Nasal + consonant

On earlier pages we have dealt with nasal consonants followed by /z/, /d/ and /θ/. Other sequences in which a nasal consonant is followed by another consonant are found in words like **sens** *sense*, **pʌntʃ** *punch*, **rɪvendʒ** *revenge*, **wɒnt** *want*, **dʒʌmp** *jump*, **θæŋk** *thank*. In all these cases the vocal organs are in exactly or almost exactly the same position for the nasal as for the second consonant; in **sens** the tongue-tip is lowered slightly at the same time as the soft palate is raised to give the /s/ friction; in all the other cases the tongue and lips remain in the same position in passing from the nasal to the following consonant. Be sure that the nasal consonant is firmly formed and not replaced by nasalizing the previous vowel (see p. 50).

In the word **traɪəmf** *triumph* the /m/-sound may be formed with the lower lip against the upper teeth, rather than with the two lips, but it is not necessary to do this unless you find it helpful.

There are plural or past forms of all the examples given above, e.g. **senst** *sensed*, **pʌntʃt** *punched*, **rɪvendʒd** *revenged*, **wɒnts** *wants*, **dʒʌmpt** *jumped*, **dʒʌmps** *jumps*, **θæŋkt** *thanked*, **θæŋks** *thanks*, **traɪəmfs** *triumphs*. Remember that with /pt/ and /kt/ the first stop is not exploded (see p. 67). Practise at these examples until you get a smooth change between the consonants.

4.3 Longer consonant sequences

In phrases one word may end with a consonant sequence and the next word may begin with one, so that longer sequences such as /ŋkskl/ quite commonly occur, for example in **ðə bæŋks kləʊzd** *the bank's closed*. As always there is a smooth passage from each consonant to the

Longer consonant sequences

next, with no gap. If you have mastered the initial and final sequences, the only difficulty will be to pass smoothly from the last consonant of the final sequence to the first of the initial sequence, with no vowel or interval between. This is done, as before, by putting the vocal organs in position for the following consonant during the previous one. The examples below will give you practice in sequences of increasing length.

Three consonants

best mæn	best man	pəhæps nɒt	perhaps not
fɪks ðɪs	fix this	help miː	help me
θæŋk juː	thank you	tʃeɪnʒ wʌn	change one
wɒtʃ krɪkɪt	watch cricket	tɔːl triː	tall tree
naɪs tjuːn	nice tune	laʊd kraɪ	loud cry
lɒŋ skɜːt	long skirt	peɪdʒ twentɪ	page twenty

Four consonants

nekst sʌndɪ	next Sunday	twelfθ naɪt	twelfth night
bɒtl̩d waɪn	bottled wine	hiː θæŋkt ðəm	he thanked them
vɑːst skeɪl	vast scale	ðæts truː	that's true
streɪndʒ driːm	strange dream	fɪfθ flɔː	fifth floor
smɔːl skweə	small square	lɒŋ striːt	long street
bɪg splæʃ	big splash	gʊd stjuːdn̩t	good student

Five consonants

mɪlks friː	milk's free	prɒmpt stɑːt	prompt start
mɪkst swiːts	mixed sweets	plɑːnts ʃrɪvl̩	plants shrivel
bent sprɪŋ	bent spring	ækt stjuːpɪdlɪ	act stupidly
bent skruː	bent screw	ðæts splendɪd	that's splendid

Six consonants

nekst sprɪŋ	next Spring	hɪndʒd skriːn	hinged screen
hiː θɪŋks streɪt	he thinks straight	aɪ helpt stjʊət	I helped Stuart
ə fenst skweə	a fenced square	twelfθ striːt	Twelfth Street

Seven consonants

ðə teksts stjuːpɪd — the text's stupid
ʃiː tempts streɪndʒəz — she tempts strangers

Consonant sequences

4.4 Exercises

1. Does your language have sequences of two, three, four or more consonants? If so, list the ones which are similar to English sequences.
2. Does your language have stop+stop sequences? Practise again the examples on p. 69.
3. Be sure that you can distinguish the following: spy, espy; state, estate; scape, escape; support, sport; succumb, scum; polite, plight; terrain, train; below, blow; strange, estrange; ascribe, scribe; esquire, squire; astute, stewed; ticket, ticked; wrapped, rapid, wrap it.
4. Does your language have nasal explosion (p. 70) or lateral explosion (p. 72)? Practise those examples again.
5. Practise again all the other examples in this chapter, being very careful to follow the instructions given. Finish with the longer sequences on p. 77.

5 The vowels of English

Vowels are made by voiced air passing through different mouth-shapes; the differences in the shape of the mouth are caused by different positions of the tongue and of the lips. It is easy to see and to feel the lip differences, but it is very difficult to see or to feel the tongue differences, and that is why a detailed description of the tongue position for a certain vowel does not really help us to pronounce it well.

Vowels must be learned by *listening and imitating:* I could tell you that the English vowel /ɔː/ as in *saw* is made by rounding the lips and by placing the back of the tongue in a position mid-way between the highest possible and the lowest possible position, but it would be much more helpful if I could simply say the sound for you and get you to imitate me. Since I cannot do this I must leave the listening and imitating to you. So spend some of your listening time on the vowels.

As I said at the beginning of chapter 3 English speakers vary quite a lot in their vowel sounds; the vowels used by an Australian, an American and a Scotsman in the word *see* are all different, but they are all recognized quite easily as /iː/. So the actual sounds that you use for the English vowels are not so important as the differences that you make between them. There must be *differences between* the vowels, and that is what we will concentrate on.

5.1 Simple vowels

/iː, ɪ, e/

In your language you will have a vowel which is like the English /iː/ in *see*, and one which is like the English /ʌ/ in *sun*, and almost certainly one which is like the English /e/ in *get*. They may not be *exactly* the same as the English vowels you hear in listening to English, but they will do for a starting-point. Say the words **biːd** *bead* and **bed** *bed* several times and listen carefully to the sound of the vowels; then try to say a vowel which is *between* the other two, and different from both, not **biːd** and not **bed**, but ... **bɪd** – that will be the vowel in *bid*. You need

Vowels

three different vowels for the three words *bead*, *bid* and *bed*. Be sure that the middle vowel *is different* and *between* the other two: one thing which will help you to distinguish /iː/ from /ɪ/ is that /iː/ is longer than /ɪ/ as well as different in the quality of the sound. Practise those three words (and listen for them in English) until you are sure that you can keep them separate. The most likely difficulty is that you will confuse /iː/ with /ɪ/, so be sure that /ɪ/ is nearer in quality to /e/ and that it is always shorter than /iː/.

Remember that when the vowels are followed by a strong consonant they are shorter than when they are followed by a weak consonant, so that *beat*, *bit* and *bet* all have shorter vowels than *bead*, *bid* and *bed*, but even so the vowel /iː/ is always longer than the vowels /ɪ/ and /e/ in any one set. Now practise the following sets and pay attention to both the length of the vowels and their quality:

liːd	lead	lɪd	lid	led	led
wiːt	wheat	wɪt	wit	wet	wet
biːn	been	bɪn	bin	ben	Ben
tʃiːk	cheek	tʃɪk	chick	tʃek	check
fiːl	feel	fɪl	fill	fel	fell
riːtʃ	reach	rɪtʃ	rich	retʃ	wretch

/e, æ, ʌ/

Now you need another vowel between /e/ and /ʌ/, that is the vowel /æ/. Say the words **bed** *bed* and **bʌd** *bud* several times and be sure that your mouth is quite wide open for the vowel of **bʌd**. Listen to the vowels carefully and then try to say a vowel which is *between* those two, a vowel which sounds a bit like /e/ and a bit like /ʌ/ but which is different from both. You *must* have different vowels in *bed*, *bad* and *bud*. Practise those three words until you can always make a difference between them; they all have comparatively short vowels so that length differences will not help you here.

Practise the following sets and be sure that each word really sounds different:

ten	ten	tæn	tan	tʌn	ton
bet	bet	bæt	bat	bʌt	but
pen	pen	pæn	pan	pʌn	pun
seks	sex	sæks	sacks	sʌks	sucks
ded	dead	dæd	Dad	dʌd	dud
meʃ	mesh	mæʃ	mash	mʌʃ	mush

Simple vowels

/iː, ɪ, e, æ, ʌ/

Now try all five of these vowels in the sets given below: you will see that there are gaps in some of the sets, where no word exists, for instance there is no word lek; but for practice you can fill in the gaps too. Some of the words are rather uncommon, but don't worry about the meanings – just be sure that the vowel sounds are different:

biːd	bead	bɪd	bid	bed	bed	bæd	bad	bʌd	bud
liːk	leak	lɪk	lick			læk	lack	lʌk	luck
hiːl	heel	hɪl	hill	hel	hell	hæl	Hal	hʌl	hull
tiːn	teen	tɪn	tin	ten	ten	tæn	tan	tʌn	ton
niːt	neat	nɪt	knit	net	net	næt	gnat	nʌt	nut
liːst	least	lɪst	list	lest	lest			lʌst	lust
riːm	ream	rɪm	rim			ræm	ram	rʌm	rum
biːt	beat	bɪt	bit	bet	bet	bæt	bat	bʌt	but

/ʌ, ɑː, ɒ/

In England when the doctor wants to look into your mouth and examine your throat he asks you to say *Ah*, that is the vowel /ɑː/, because for this vowel the tongue is very low and he can see over it to the back of the palate and the pharynx. So if you have no vowel exactly like /ɑː/ in your language you may find a mirror useful – keep your mouth wide open and play with various vowel sounds until you find one which allows you to see the very back of the soft palate quite clearly; this will be similar to an English /ɑː/, but you must compare it with the /ɑː/ vowels that you hear when you listen to English and adjust your sound if necessary. Remember that /ɑː/ is a long vowel. The short vowel /ɒ/ is a bit like /ɑː/ in quality though of course they must be kept separate. For /ɒ/ the lips may be slightly rounded, for /ɑː/ they are not. Try the following sets:

lʌk	luck	lɑːk	lark	lɒk	lock
kʌd	cud	kɑːd	card	kɒd	cod
dʌk	duck	dɑːk	dark	dɒk	dock
lʌst	lust	lɑːst	last	lɒst	lost
bʌks	bucks	bɑːks	barks	bɒks	box
kʌp	cup	kɑːp	carp	kɒp	cop

/ɒ, ɔː, ʊ, uː/

In your language there will be a vowel which is similar to the English

Vowels

/uː/ in *two*. The /uː/ in English, like /iː/ and /ɑː/, is always longer than the other vowels. Between /ɒ/ and /uː/ you need to make two other vowels, /ɔː/, a long one, as in /lɔː/ *law*, and /ʊ/, a short one, as in pʊt *put*. For /ɔː/ the mouth is less open than for /ɒ/ and the lips are more rounded, but /ɔː/ is nearer in quality to /ɒ/ than to /uː/. For /ʊ/ the lips are also rounded, but the sound is nearer in quality to /uː/. All four vowels, /ɒ, ɔː, ʊ, uː/, must be kept separate, and the differences of length will help in this. Try the following sets:

ʃɒd	shod	ʃɔːd	shored	ʃʊd	should	ʃuːd	shoed
kɒd	cod	kɔːd	cord	kʊd	could	kuːd	cooed
wɒd	wad	wɔːd	ward	wʊd	would	wuːd	wooed
lɒk	lock			lʊk	look	luːk	Luke
pɒl	Poll	pɔːl	Paul	pʊl	pull	puːl	pool

/ɜː, ɑː/

The vowel /ɜː/ as in /hɜː/ *her* is a long vowel which is not very close in quality to any of the other vowels and usually sounds rather vague and indistinct to the foreign learner. You must listen to the vowel especially carefully and try to imitate the indistinctness of it (though to an English listener it sounds quite distinct!). Two things will help: keep your teeth quite close together and do not round your lips at all – smile when you say it! The two commonest mistakes with /ɜː/ are, first, to replace it by /er/ or by some vowel in your own language which has lip-rounding but which is not likely to be confused with any other English vowel, and second, and more important, it is replaced by /ɑː/ by Japanese speakers and speakers of many African languages and others. In the first case there is no danger of misunderstanding although the vowel will sound strange; in the second case there is danger of misunderstanding, since words like hɜːt *hurt* and hɑːt *heart* will be confused.

In your listening-time pay special attention to /ɜː/ and experiment (always with teeth close together and a smile on your face) until you approach the right quality; then make sure that you can distinguish it from /ɑː/ – which has the teeth further apart – in the following pairs:

pɜːs	purse	pɑːs	pass	bɜːn	burn	bɑːn	barn
hɜːd	heard	hɑːd	hard	fɜːm	firm	fɑːm	farm
pɜːtʃt	perched	pɑːtʃt	parched	lɜːks	lurks	lɑːks	larks

/ə/

The vowel /ə/ in bənɑːnə *banana* is the commonest of the English

Simple vowels

vowels and is a short version of /ɜː/. It is particularly short and indistinct when it is not final, e.g. in əgen *again*, kəntein *contain*, pəʊstmən *postman*. In final position, that is before a pause, as in betə *better*, eiʃə *Asia*, kɒlə *collar*, the vowel sounds more like /ʌ/, though it is not usually so clear.

There are two main difficulties with this vowel: first, to identify it, that is, to know when it is this vowel you should be aiming at; and second, to get the right quality. In the first case, do not be deceived by English spelling: there is no single letter which always stands for this vowel, so rely on your ear – listen very carefully and you will hear dozens of examples of /ə/ in every bit of English you listen to. In the second case, it is often useful to think of leaving out the vowel altogether in words such as kəndem *condemn*, sætədı *Saturday*, dʒent|mən *gentleman*, where /ə/ comes between consonants. Of course, you will not really leave out the vowel, but you will have a minimum vowel and that is what /ə/ is. Then in initial position, as in ətempt *attempt*, əkaʊnt *account*, əbzɜːv *observe*, you must again keep it very short and very obscure. But in final position it need not be so short and it may be more like /ʌ/, with the mouth a little more open than in other positions.

Try the following examples:

In medial position

pəhæps	perhaps	kəntein	contain
entəteın	entertain	ımbærəs	embarrass
dınəz	dinners	hındəd	hindered
æmətɜː	amateur	glæmərəs	glamorous
kʌmfətəb|	comfortable	kəmpəʊnənt	component
ıgnərənt	ignorant	kærəktəz	characters
ʌndəstænd	understand	menəs	menace
paılət	pilot	terəb|	terrible
pɜːmənənt	permanent	kəreıdʒəs	courageous

In initial position

əbeı	obey	ətend	attend
əlaʊ	allow	əbstrʌkt	obstruct
əmaʊnt	amount	ətʃiːv	achieve
ədɔː	adore	əkaʊnt	account
ənɔı	annoy	əsaıd	aside
əpruːv	approve	əgriː	agree

Vowels

əpɪə appear ədʒɜːn adjourn
əfens offence

In final position

suːnə	sooner	seɪlə	sailor
meʒə	measure	kɒlə	collar
sʌlfə	sulphur	ʃəʊfə	chauffeur
æfrɪkə	Africa	əmerɪkə	America
pɜːʃə	Persia	kænədə	Canada
flætərə	flatterer	ədmaɪərə	admirer
kʌlə	colour	zefə	zephyr
pɪktʃə	picture	tʃaɪnə	China
mɜːdərə	murderer	kəmpəʊzə	composer

More examples of /ə/ will be found in the next chapter when we consider the *weak forms* of certain words, such as *at* and *for* in ət taɪmz *at times* and fə juː *for you*.

5.2 Diphthongs

A diphthong is a glide from one vowel to another, and the whole glide acts like one of the long, simple vowels; so we have biː, ɑː, ɔː and also beɪ, bəʊ, baɪ, baʊ, bɔɪ, bɪə, beə, bʊə. The diphthongs of English are in three groups: those which end in /ʊ/, /əʊ, aʊ/, those which end in /ɪ/, /eɪ, aɪ, ɔɪ/, and those which end in /ə/, /ɪə, eə, ʊə/.

/əʊ, aʊ/

Both these diphthongs end with /ʊ/ rather than /uː/ although you will not be misunderstood if you do use /uː/. To get /əʊ/ as in səʊ *so*, start with /ɜː/ and then glide away to /ʊ/ with the lips getting slightly rounded and the sound becoming less loud as the glide progresses. Be sure that the first part of the diphthong is /ɜː/ (a real English /ɜː/!) and not /ɔː/ or anything like it, and be sure that the sound *is* a diphthong, not a simple vowel of the /ɔː/ type. /əʊ/ and /ɔː/ must be kept quite separate. Try the following:

ləʊ	low	lɔː	law	səʊ	so	sɔː	saw
snəʊ	snow	snɔː	snore	bəʊt	boat	bɔːt	bought
kləʊz	close	klɔːz	claws	kəʊk	coke	kɔːk	cork
kəʊl	coal	kɔːl	call				

Diphthongs

For /aʊ/ start with /ʌ/. Say tʌn *ton*, and then after the /ʌ/-sound add an /ʊ/; this should give taʊn *town*. /aʊ/ is not difficult for most people. Be sure that /aʊ/ and /əʊ/ are different. Try the following:

naʊ	now	nəʊ	know
laʊd	loud	ləʊd	load
faʊnd	found	fəʊnd	phoned
raʊ	row (quarrel)	rəʊ	row (line)
daʊt	doubt	dəʊt	dote
taʊnz	towns	təʊnz	tones

Remember when you practise these examples that diphthongs are shorter before strong consonants and longer before weak ones, just like the other vowels, so bəʊt *boat* has a shorter diphthong than kləʊz *close* and daʊt *doubt* a shorter one than laʊd *loud*. Go back over all those examples and get the lengths right. When no consonant follows, as in ləʊ *low*, the diphthong is at its longest.

/eɪ, aɪ, ɔɪ/

These diphthongs all end in /ɪ/, not /iː/ (though it is not serious if you do use /iː/ finally). /eɪ/ begins with /e/ as in *men*. Say men and then add /ɪ/ after /e/, gliding smoothly from /e/ to /ɪ/ and making the sound less loud as the glide progresses – this will give meɪn *main*. The most common mistake is to use a long, simple vowel, so try to be sure that there is a glide from /e/ to /ɪ/; however, if you do use a simple vowel for /eɪ/ it will not be misunderstood – some accents of English (e.g. Scottish) do the same. But /eɪ/ and /e/ must be quite separate. Try the following:

leɪt	late	let	let	seɪl	sail	sel	sell
peɪpə	paper	pepə	pepper	treɪd	trade	tred	tread
reɪk	rake	rek	wreck	feɪl	fail	fel	fell

/aɪ/ glides from /ʌ/ to /ɪ/, and the loudness becomes less as the glide progresses. Say fʌn *fun*, and then add /ɪ/ after the /ʌ/, with a smooth glide; this will give you faɪn *fine*. Be sure that /aɪ/ is separate from /eɪ/:

waɪt	white	weɪt	wait	laɪd	lied	leɪd	laid
raɪs	rice	reɪs	race	raɪz	rise	reɪz	raise
laɪk	like	leɪk	lake	faɪl	file	feɪl	fail

/ɔɪ/ glides from /ɔː/ to /ɪ/, and as usual the loudness becomes less during

Vowels

the glide. Say dʒɔː *jaw* and then add /ɪ/, as before. This will give you /dʒɔɪ/ *joy*. The /ɔː/ sound is not as long in /ɔɪ/ as it is when it is alone, as in /dʒɔː/. /ɔɪ/ is not a very common diphthong and it is not likely to be confused with any other vowel or diphthong. Try these words:

bɔɪ	boy	tɔɪ	toy	ənɔɪ	annoy	nɔɪz	noise
ɔɪl	oil	dʒɔɪn	join	əvɔɪd	avoid	bɔɪlz	boils
vɔɪs	voice	hɔɪst	hoist	dʒɔɪnt	joint	lɔɪtə	loiter

/ɪə, eə, ʊə/

These are all glides to the sort of /ə/-sound found in final position, as described on p. 83. /ɪə/ glides from /ɪ/ (not /iː/) to this /ə/ in words like hɪə *hear*, nɪə *near*, etc. If you do use /iː/ at the beginning of the glide it will sound a bit strange but you will not be misunderstood. Try the following:

ɪə	ear	jɪə	year	bɪə	beer	klɪə	clear
fɪə	fear	rɪəl	real	bɪəd	beard	aɪdɪəz	ideas
kərɪən	Korean	fɪəs	fierce	pɪəs	pierce	nɪərə	nearer
rɪəlɪ	really						

Words such as fʌnɪə *funnier* and glɔːrɪəs *glorious*, where /ɪə/ is the result of adding an ending /ə/ or /əs/ to a word which ends with /ɪ/, should be pronounced in the same way as the /ɪə/ in *hear*, *near*, etc. The same is true for words such as ɪndɪə *India*, eərɪə *area*, juːnɪən *union*, etc.

To make /eə/, start with the word hæz *has* (with the proper English /æ/, between /e/ and /ʌ/) and then add /ʌ/ after the /æ/, gliding smoothly from /æ/ to /ʌ/; this will give you the word heəz *hairs*. Notice that the beginning of the diphthong is /æ/ rather than /e/. You must keep /ɪə/ and /eə/ quite separate; try the following:

hɪə	here	heə	hair	bɪə	beer	beə	bare
stɪəd	steered	steəd	stared	ɪəz	ears	eəz	airs
rɪəlɪ	really	reəlɪ	rarely	wɪərɪ	weary	weərɪ	wary

/ʊə/ starts from /ʊ/ (not /uː/) and glides to /ə/; if you use /uː/ at the beginning of the glide it will sound a bit strange but you will not be misunderstood. Try the following:

pʊə	poor	ɪnʃʊərəns	insurance
ʃʊəlɪ	surely	kjʊərɪɒsətɪ	curiosity
fjʊərɪəs	furious	kjʊə	cure

Diphthongs

pjʊə	pure	tʊərɪst	tourist
ʃʊə	sure	pjʊəlɪ	purely

All these words may also be pronounced with /ɔː/ instead of /ʊə/ in R.P., /pɔː, ʃɔː, kjɔː/, etc. Other words, like *fewer, bluer, continuous*, are also usually pronounced with /ʊə/ – fjʊə, blʊə, kəntɪnjʊəs – though they can always be pronounced with /uːə/ – fjuːə, bluːə, kəntɪnjuːəs – and in any case they must not be pronounced with /ɔː/. This is also true for *cruel* and *jewel* which must have either /ʊə/ or /uːə/.

5.3 Vowel sequences

There are vowel sequences as well as consonant sequences but they are not so difficult. In general, when one vowel (or diphthong) follows another you should pronounce each one quite normally but with a smooth glide between them. The most common sequences are formed by adding /ə/ to a diphthong, especially to /aɪ/ and /aʊ/ in words like faɪə *fire* and aʊə *our*. When you listen to these two sequences – /aɪə, aʊə/ – you will notice that the /ɪ/ in *fire* and the /ʊ/ in *our* are rather weak; in fact both sequences may sound rather like /ɑː/. It is probably best for you not to imitate this but to pronounce the sequences as /aɪ + ə/ and /aʊ + ə/, though the /ɪ/ and the /ʊ/ should not be made too strong. Try the following:

taɪə	tyre	taʊə	tower
traɪəl	trial	traʊəl	trowel
kwaɪət	quiet	taɪəd	tired
kaʊəd	coward	paʊəfʊl	powerful
baɪə	buyer	baʊə	bower
flaɪə	flyer	flaʊə	flower
aɪən	iron	raɪət	riot
aʊəz	ours	ʃaʊərɪ	showery

The less common sequences /eɪə, əʊə, ɔɪə/ should be pronounced with the normal diphthong smoothly followed by /ə/. The /ɪ/ and /ʊ/ need not be weakened at all. Try:

greɪə	greyer	ɪmplɔɪə	employer
grəʊə	grower	θrəʊə	thrower
pleɪə	player	bɪtreɪəl	betrayal
rɔɪəl	royal	lɔɪəz	lawyers
fɒləʊəz	followers		

Vowels

/iː/ and /uː/ are also followed by /ə/ in words like *freer* and *bluer* which may be pronounced friːə or frɪə, and bluːə or blʊə, as we have seen.

The verb ending *-ing* /ɪŋ/ gives various sequences in words like the following:

biːɪŋ	being	siːɪŋ	seeing
duːɪŋ	doing	stjuːɪŋ	stewing
əlaʊɪŋ	allowing	baʊɪŋ	bowing
drɔːɪŋ	drawing	sɔːɪŋ	sawing
gəʊɪŋ	going	nəʊɪŋ	knowing

In words like *saying, enjoying, flying*, where *-ing* follows a word ending with /eɪ/, /ɔɪ/ or /aɪ/, it is common to pronounce seɪŋ, ɪndʒɔɪŋ, flaɪŋ, if you find this easier.

In words like *carrying, pitying*, etc., where a word which ends with /ɪ/ has /ɪŋ/ added to it, it is usual (and best for you) to pronounce kæriːɪŋ, pɪtiːɪŋ, etc., although kærɪ and pɪtɪ are the normal forms.

Other vowel sequences are found both within words and between words. These also should be performed with a smooth glide between the vowels. (See also p. 101.) Here are some examples:

keɪɒs	chaos	rʊɪn	ruin
bɪɒnd	beyond	rɪækt	react
bluːɪʃ	bluish	greɪ aɪd	grey-eyed
ðiː end	the end	maɪ əʊn	my own

baɪɒgrəfɪ	biography
kəʊɒpəreɪt	co-operate
juː ɑːnt	you aren't
gəʊ aʊt	go out

| tuː aʊəz | two hours |
| meɪ aɪ əʊ ɪt tuː juː | may I owe it to you? |

5.4 Exercises

(Answers, where appropriate, on p. 135)

1. What vowels and diphthongs do you have in your language? Which of the English ones cause you difficulty?
2. During your listening-time listen carefully to one of the difficult vowels at a time and try to get the sound of it into your head. Make a list of twenty words containing each difficult vowel and practise them.

Exercises

3 Go back and practise all the examples given in this chapter, and concentrate on making *differences* between the different vowels.
4 Is the length of vowels important in your language? Practise making the difference between the long vowels (including the diphthongs) and the short vowels of English. Don't forget that vowel length is affected by following strong and weak consonants; complete the following list for all the vowels and practise it, thinking about vowel length:
bi:d   bi:t
hɪz   hɪs
sed   set
5 Make a list of phrases like the ones on p. 88, where a vowel or diphthong at the end of one word is immediately followed by another at the beginning of the next. Practise saying them smoothly, with no break between the vowels.

6 Words in company

6.1 Word groups and stress

When we talk we do not talk in single words but in groups of words spoken continuously, with no break or pause; we may pause after a group, but not during it. These groups may be long, for example, *However did you manage to do it so neatly and tidily?*, or they may be short, as when we say simply *Yes* or *No*, or they may be of intermediate length, like *How did you do it?* or *Come over here a minute*. When we have longer things to say we break them up into manageable groups like this: ||*Last Wednesday* | *I wanted to get up to London early* || *so I caught a train* | *about half an hour before my usual one* || *and I got to work* | *about half past eight*||.

When one group is very closely connected grammatically to the next, there is a very slight pause, marked by (|). When two groups are not so closely connected, there is a longer pause, marked by (||), and this double bar is also used to mark the end of a complete utterance. It is not usually difficult to see how a long utterance can be broken up into shorter groups, but when you listen to English notice how the speakers do it both in reading and in conversation.

In the group *I could hardly believe my eyes* the words *hardly*, *believe* and *eyes* are stressed: this means that one of the syllables of the word (the only syllable in *eyes*!) is said with greater force, with greater effort, than the others; in *hardly* it is the first syllable /hɑːd-/, and in *believe* it is the second syllable /-liːv/. All the remaining syllables in the group are said more weakly, they are *unstressed*; only /hɑːd-/, /-liːv/ and /aɪz/ have the extra effort or *stress*. We can show this by placing the mark * immediately *before* the syllables which have stress, for example:

||aɪ kʊd *hɑːdlɪ bɪ*liːv maɪ *aɪz||

Hardly always has stress on the first syllable, never on the second, and *believe* always has stress on the second syllable, never on the first; every English word has a definite place for the stress and we are not allowed

Word groups and stress

to change it. The first syllable is the most common place for the stress, as in *father, any, steadily, gathering, excellently, obstinacy, reasonableness;* many words are stressed on the second syllable, like *about, before, attractive, beginning, intelligent, magnificently.* Some words have *two* stressed syllables, for example, *fourteen* *fɔː*tiːn, *half-hearted* *hɑːf*hɑːtɪd, *disbelieve* *dɪsbɪ*liːv, *contradiction* *kɒntrə*dɪkʃən, *qualification* *kwɒlɪfɪ*keɪʃən, *examination* ɪg*zæmɪ*neɪʃən, *terrified* *terɪ*faɪd, *indicate* *ɪndɪ*keɪt.

6.2 Stressed and unstressed syllables

There is no simple way of knowing which syllable or syllables in an English word must be stressed, but every time you learn another word you must be sure to learn how it is stressed: any good dictionary of English will give you this information. If you stress the wrong syllable it spoils the shape of the word for an English hearer and he may have difficulty in recognizing the word.

As we saw in the group *I could hardly believe my eyes* not all words are stressed; *I* and *could* and *my* are unstressed. What sort of words are stressed, then, and what sort are unstressed? First, all words of more than one syllable are stressed. In some circumstances English speakers do not stress such words, but it is always possible to stress them and you should do so. Next, words of one syllable are generally *not* stressed if they are purely grammatical words like pronouns (*I, me, you, he, she,* etc.), prepositions (*to, for, at, from, by,* etc.), articles (*the, a, an, some*). Other words are stressed, for example, full verbs (*eat, love, take, try,* etc.), nouns (*head, chair, book, pen,* etc.), adjectives (*good, blue, long, cold,* etc.), adverbs (*well, just, quite, not*) and the like. In general it is the picture words which are stressed, the words which give us the picture or provide most of the information. We shall see later that for special purposes it is possible to stress any English word, even the purely grammatical ones, but usually they are unstressed.

Syllables which are not stressed often contain the vowel /ə/ instead of any clearer vowel, and this vowel /ə/ only occurs in unstressed syllables, *never* in stressed ones. For instance, in all the examples on p. 83 the /ə/ is in an unstressed syllable. In the word *contain* kən*teɪn the second syllable is stressed and the first has /ə/, but in the noun *contents* *kɒntents the first syllable is stressed and has the clearer vowel /ɒ/. Here are some examples of the same kind; say them with the effort on the correct syllable and with the right vowels:

    əb*teɪn   obtain   *ɒbdʒɪkt   object (n.)

Words in company

pə*mɪt	permit (v.)	*pɜːfɪkt	perfect (adj.)
prə*vaɪd	provide	*prəʊgres	progress (n.)
*fəʊtə*grɑːf	photograph	fə*tɒgrəfɪ	photography
prɪ*peə	prepare	*prepə*reɪʃən	preparation
kəm*baɪn	combine (v.)	*kɒmbɪ*neɪʃən	combination
*kɒnvənt	convent	ɪn*vent	invent

But it is not true, as you can see, that /ə/ is the only vowel which occurs in unstressed syllables; all the other vowels can occur there too and /ɪ/ is commonly found there, the remaining vowels less commonly so. Here are examples of other vowels in unstressed syllables; say them as before:

*plentɪ	plenty	*enɪθɪŋ	anything
*hɪkʌp	hiccough	juː*tɪlɪtɪ	utility
*θæŋkjʊ	thank you	*wɪndəʊ	window
trænz*leɪt	translate	meɪn*teɪn	maintain
dɪ*saɪd	decide	vaɪ*breɪt	vibrate
ɔː*spɪʃəs	auspicious	*gærɑːʒ	garage

6.3 Weak forms of words

In *It was too expensive for them to buy* the words *too, expensive* and *buy* are stressed, giving ɪt wəz *tuː ɪk*spensɪv fə ðəm tə *baɪ. Notice the pronunciation of the words *was, for, them* and *to;* all of them have the vowel /ə/. If those words are pronounced alone, they have the pronunciations wɒz, fɔː, ðem and tuː, but usually they are not pronounced alone and usually they are not stressed, and then the forms with /ə/ are used; we call these the *weak forms* of those words.

English people often think that when they use these weak forms they are being rather careless in their speech and believe that it would be more correct always to use the strong forms, like wɒz, tuː, etc. This is not true, and English spoken with only strong forms sounds wrong. The use of weak forms is an essential part of English speech and you must learn to use the weak forms of 35 English words if you want your English to *sound* English. Some words have more than one weak form and the following list tells you when to use one and when the other:

Word	Weak form	Examples
and	ən	*blæk ən *waɪt
as	əz	əz *gʊd əz *gəʊld
but	bət	bət *waɪ *nɒt?

Weak forms of words

than	ðən	*betə ðən *evə
that	ðət	aɪ əd*mɪt ðət aɪ *dɪd ɪt
	(The word *that* in phrases like *that man, that's good* is always pronounced ðæt and *never* weakened.)	
he	iː	*dɪd iː *wɪn?
him	ɪm	*gɪv ɪm *tuː
his	ɪz	aɪ *laɪk ɪz *taɪ
her	ɜː	*teɪk ɜː *həʊm
	(At the beginning of word groups the forms hiː, hɪm, hɪz, hɜː should be used: hiː *laɪks ɪt, hɜː *feɪs ɪz *red)	
them	ðəm	*send ðəm baɪ *pəʊst
us	s (only in *let's*)	*lets *duː ɪt *naʊ
	əs	hiː *wɒʊnt *let əs *duːɪt
do	də	*haʊ də ðeɪ *nəʊ?
	(də is only used before consonants. Before vowels, use the strong form duː: *haʊ duː *aɪ*nəʊ?)	
does	dəz	*wen dəz ðə *treɪn *liːv?
am	m (after *I*)	aɪ m *taɪəd.
	əm (elsewhere)	*wen əm aɪ tə *biː *ðeə?
are	ə (before consonants)	ðə *gɜːlz ə *bjuːtəfl̩
	ər (before vowels)	ðə *men ər *ʌglɪ
be	bɪ	*dəʊnt bɪ *ruːd
is	s (after /p, t, k, f, θ/)	*ðæt s *faɪn
	z (after vowels and voiced consonants except /z, ʒ, dʒ/)	*weə z *dʒɒn?
		*dʒɒn z *hɪə
	(After /s, z, ʃ, ʒ, tʃ, dʒ/ the strong form ɪz is always used: *wɪtʃ ɪz *raɪt?)	
was	wəz	ðə *weðə wəz *terəbl̩!
has	əz (after /s, z, ʃ, ʒ, tʃ, dʒ/)	ðə *pleɪs əz *tʃeɪndʒd
	s (after /p, t, k, f, θ/)	*dʒæk s *gɒn
	z (elsewhere)	*dʒɒn z biːn *sɪk
have	v (after *I, we, you, they*)	juː v *brəʊkən ɪt
	əv (elsewhere)	ðə *men əv *gɒn

Words in company

had	d (after *I, he, she, we, you, they*)	ðeɪd *left *həʊm
	əd (elsewhere)	ðə *deɪ əd biːn *faɪn
	(At the beginning of word groups the forms hæz, hæv, hæd should be used: hæz *enɪwʌn *faʊnd? When *has, have, had* are full verbs they should always be pronounced hæz, hæv, hæd: aɪ hæv *tu: *brʌðəz)	
can	kən	*haʊ kən aɪ *help?
shall	ʃļ	aɪ ʃļ bɪ *krɒs
will	l (after *I, he, she, we, you, they*)	ðeɪ l *gɪv ɪt ə*weɪ
	ļ (after consonants, except /l/)	*ðɪs ļ *duː
	əl (after vowels and /l/)	ðə *bɔɪ əl *luːz ən ðə *gɜːl əl *wɪn
would	d (after *I, he, she, we, you, they*)	*aɪ d *duː ɪt
	əd (elsewhere)	*dʒɒn əd *duː ɪt
must	məst	aɪ məst *tel ɪm
a	ə (before consonants)	ə *paʊnd ə *deɪ
an	ən (before vowels)	*hæv ən *æpļ
the	ðə (before consonants)	ðə *mɔː ðə *merɪə
	(Before vowels the strong form ðiː should be used: ðiː *aːnts ən ðiː *ʌŋkļz)	
some	səm	aɪ *niːd səm *peɪpə
	(When *some* means 'a certain quantity' it is always stressed and therefore pronounced sʌm: *sʌm əv maɪ *frendz)	
at	ət	*kʌm ət *wʌns
for	fə (before consonants)	*kʌm fə *tiː
	fər (before vowels)	*kʌm fər ə *miːl
from	frəm	aɪ *sent ɪt frəm *lʌndən
of	əv	ðə *kwiːn əv *ɪŋglənd
to	tə (before consonants)	tə *steɪ ɔː tə *gəʊ
	(Before vowels the strong form tuː should be used: aɪ *wɒntɪd tuː *aːsk juː)	

Weak forms of words

The word *not* has the weak forms /nt/ (after vowels) and /n̩t/ (after consonants) when it follows *are, is, should, would, has, have, could, dare, might*. Examples: ðeɪ *ɑːnt *kʌmɪŋ; hiː *hæzn̩t ə*raɪvd. Notice especially the forms *can't* kɑːnt, *shan't* ʃɑːnt, *don't* dəʊnt, *won't* wəʊnt, *mustn't* mʌsn̩t, in which *can, shall, do, will, must* are changed when they combine with *not*. Practise all the examples given here and be sure that the weak forms are really weak, then make up similar examples for yourself and practise those too.

6.4 The use of strong forms

As I have said, the 35 common words which have weak forms also have strong forms, which *must* be used in the following cases:

1 Whenever the word is stressed, as it may be: *kæn aɪ?, *duː ðeɪ?, *hæv juː *fɪnɪʃt?, juː məst *tʃuːz *ʌs ɔː *ðem, *hiː *laɪks *hɜː bət dəz *ʃiː *laɪk *hɪm?
2 Whenever the word is *final* in the group: *dʒɒn hæz, *meərɪ wɪl, *juː ɑː, aɪ *dəʊnt *wɒnt tuː, *wɒts *ðæt fɔː?

Exceptions: he, him, his, her, them, us have their *weak* forms in final position (unless they are stressed of course): aɪ *təʊld ɜː, ʃiː *laɪks ðəm, wiː *kɔːld fər ɪm, ðeɪ *lɑːft ət əs.

not has its weak form finally when attached to *can, have, is*, etc.: *dʒɒn *kɑːnt, *meərɪ *ɪzn̩t; but never otherwise: aɪ *həʊp nɒt.

Some of the 35 words are very rarely either stressed or final in the group and so very rarely have their strong form, for example, *than, a, the*. But occasionally they are stressed for reasons of meaning and then they naturally have their strong form: aɪ sed *eɪ *sʌn, *nɒt *ðiː *sʌn (I said *a* son, not *the* sun).

Practise all these examples and then make up others for yourself and practise those too.

6.5 Rhythm units

Within the word group there is at least one stressed syllable (||*wen?|| ||*suːn|| ||*naʊ?|| ||*jes||). The length of the syllable in a very short 'group' of this kind depends on the natural length of the vowel and the following consonant(s), if any.

/naʊ/ is a very long syllable because it has a diphthong and no following consonant – we stretch it out.

/suːn/ is also very long because it has a long vowel followed by a weak consonant.

Words in company

/wen/ is a little shorter because it has a short vowel, but not *very* short because of the slight lengthening effect of the following weak consonant.

/jes/ is the shortest of these syllables because it has a short vowel followed by a strong consonant, but notice that even this kind of syllable is not *very* short in English.

The stressed syllable may have one or more unstressed syllables before it:

||ɪts *kəʊld|| ||aɪ ə*griː|| ||aɪ ʃ| kəm*pleɪn||

These unstressed syllables before the stress are said very quickly, so they are all very short, as short as you can make them; but the stressed syllable is as long as before, so there is a great difference of length between the unstressed syllables and the stressed one. Say those examples with very quick, very short unstressed syllables, and then stretch out the stressed one. Do the same with these:

aɪ m *hɪə   aɪ wəz *hɪə   aɪ wəz ɪn *hɪə
ʃiːz *həʊm   ʃiːz ət *həʊm   bət ʃiːz ət *həʊm
ðeɪ *wɜːk   ðeɪ kən *wɜːk   ðeɪ wər ət *wɜːk
wiːl *siː   wiː ʃ| *siː   ən wiː ʃ| *siː

The stressed syllable may also be followed by one or more unstressed syllables:

||*teɪkɪt|| ||*ɔːl əv ɪt?|| ||*nætʃərəlɪ||

But these unstressed syllables are not said specially quickly; what happens is that the stressed syllable and the following unstressed syllable(s) share the amount of time which a single stressed syllable would have; so

*naɪn   *naɪntɪ   *naɪntɪəθ

all take about the same time to say; naɪn is stretched out, but the naɪn in naɪntɪ is only half as long and the naɪn in naɪntɪəθ is shorter still, and the unstressed syllables are of the same length as the stressed ones; these unstressed syllables *after* the stress must not be rushed, as the ones *before* the stress are, but must be given the same amount of time as the stressed syllable. Say those examples, and be sure that the three words all take about the same time to say. Then try these:

*gʊd   *betə   *eksələnt
*faɪn   *faɪn| *faɪnəlɪ

Rhythm units

```
*wɪl        *wɪlɪŋ       *wɪlɪŋnɪs
*wɪt        *wɪtnɪs      *wɪtnɪsɪz
*drɪŋk      *drɪŋkɪŋ     *drɪŋkɪŋ ɪt
*miːt       *miːtɪŋ      *miːtɪŋ ðəm
```

In the group ||ɪt wəz *betə|| there are two unstressed syllables before the stress and one after it. The first two are said quickly, the last one not so quickly, taking the same amount of time as /be-/. Practise that group, with the first two syllables very short and the next two longer. Do the same with the following:

```
juː kən *siː ðəm                aɪ wəz ɪn *lʌndən
ðeɪ ɪn*dʒɔɪd ɪt                 ʃiː ɪk*spektɪd ɪt
hiː kʊd əv ə*vɔɪdɪd ɪt          ɪt wəz ə *mɪrək|
ɪt wəz ən *æksɪdənt             maɪ ə*pɒlədʒɪz
bət ðeə wə *plentɪ əv ðəm       jɔːr ɪm*pɒsəb|
```

The group ||*waɪ *nɒt?|| has two stresses and the two syllables are given the same length. In ||*waɪ *nɒt *gəʊ?|| the three stressed syllables are also equal in length. But in ||*waɪ *nɒt *teɪk ɪt?|| the first two syllables *waɪ *nɒt are equal in length but the following two syllables *teɪk ɪt are said in the same time as *waɪ, so they are both only half the length of *waɪ and *nɒt. This is exactly what happens with *naɪn and *naɪntɪ as we saw on p. 96. We could show this as follows:

||*waɪ *nɒt|| ||*waɪ *nɒt *gəʊ|| ||*waɪ *nɒt *teɪk ɪt||

Similarly in ||*ðæts *kwaɪt *plezn̩t|| the two syllables of *plezn̩t have the same amount of time as the single syllable *ðæts or *kwaɪt and are therefore only half as long.

||*ðæts *kwaɪt *plezn̩t||

In ||*dʒɒnz *eldɪst *sʌn|| the stressed syllables *dʒɒnz and *sʌn which are *not* followed by an unstressed syllable are of the same length, and the two syllables of *eldɪst share this same length of time between them.

||*dʒɒnz *eldɪst *sʌn||

In ||*bəʊθ əv ðəm *keɪm *bæk|| the *three* syllables *bəʊθ əv ðəm are said in the same amount of time as *keɪm or *bæk.

||*bəʊθ əv ðəm *keɪm *bæk||

Words in company

In ||*bəʊθ əv ðəm *left *ɜːlɪ|| the three syllables of *bəʊθ əv ðəm and the two syllables of *ɜːlɪ are said in the same amount of time as the single syllable *left, so *left is the longest syllable, the two syllables of *ɜːlɪ are shorter and the three of *bəʊθ əv ðəm are shorter still.

||*b<u>əʊθ</u> <u>əv</u> <u>ðəm</u> *<u>left</u> *<u>ɜːlɪ</u>||

A stressed syllable together with any unstressed syllables which may follow it form a *stress group*. So *bəʊθ əv ðəm is one stress group, *left is another and *ɜːlɪ is another. The fundamental rule of English rhythm is this: *each stress group within a word group is given the same amount of time.*

If we leave out any spaces between syllables belonging to the same stress group it will remind us that they belong to a single stress group and must be said in the same time as other stress groups in the same word group:

||*bəʊθəvðəm *left *ɜːlɪ||

Do this for the following examples:

*letɪm *teɪkɪt
*teɪkjɔː *hætɒf
*dəʊntteɪk *tuːmʌtʃ *taɪm
*ɪzʃiː *gəʊɪŋɒn *mʌndɪ?
*wɒzn̩tɪt *wʌndəflɪ *kaɪndəvɪm?
*sendðəm *leɪtə
*nʌnəvəs *laɪktɪt *ðeə
*meɪaɪ *bɒrəʊɪt *naʊ?
*hævjuː *hɜːdhaʊ *dʒɒnɪz?
*breɪkɪtɪntə *sevrəl *piːsɪz

Now practise those examples; the best way is to beat the rhythm with your hand, one beat for each stressed syllable and with exactly the same time between each pair of beats. I find it useful to bang rhythmically on the table with my pen, and at each bang comes a stressed syllable; you try it too. And don't forget that each stress group gets the same time as the others in that word group, and that each syllable in the stress group gets the same time as the others in that stress group.

In the group ||aɪm *gəʊɪŋ *həʊm|| there are two stress groups *gəʊɪŋ and *həʊm. The syllable aɪm does not belong to any stress group since it comes *before* the stress, and it is said very quickly, as we

Rhythm units

saw earlier, quicker than the unstressed syllable in the stress group *gəʊɪŋ. We can show this as follows:

||aɪm *gəʊɪŋ *həʊm||

In the group ||aɪm *gəʊɪŋ *həʊm tə*deɪ|| the unstressed syllable /tə-/ in tə*deɪ behaves exactly like aɪm, it is said very quickly, and the stressed syllable *həʊm is still just as long as the two syllables of *gəʊɪŋ, not reduced in length as you might expect:

||aɪm *gəʊɪŋ *həʊm tə*deɪ||

So we say that /tə-/ does *not* belong to the same stress group as həʊm but that it is outside any stress group, like aɪm. Exactly the same is true for fə in ||aɪm *gəʊɪŋ *həʊm fə *krɪsməs||

||aɪm *gəʊɪŋ *həʊm fə *krɪsməs||

We say that these very quick, very short syllables come *before* the stress, and we might write these examples like this:

||aɪm*gəʊɪŋ *həʊm tə*deɪ||
||aɪm*gəʊɪŋ *həʊm fə*krɪsməs||

In this sort of arrangement any unstressed syllable *before* the stressed syllable is said very quickly and does not affect the length of syllables before it. We say them as quickly as we can so that they interfere as little as possible with the regular return of the stressed syllables. Any unstressed syllable *after* the stress is of course part of the stress group and shares the available time with the other syllables of the stress group.

A unit of this kind, with a stressed syllable as its centre and any unstressed syllables which may come *before* it and *after* it, is called a *rhythm unit*. So aɪm*gəʊɪŋ is a rhythm unit, and so is *həʊm and so is fə*krɪsməs.

How do you decide what words or syllables go together in a rhythm unit? Here are the rules:

1 Any unstressed syllables at the beginning of a word group must go together with the following stress group:

||aɪwəzɪn*lʌndən|| ||maɪə*pɒlədʒɪz||

2 If the unstressed syllable(s) is part of the same word as the stressed syllable they belong to the same rhythm group:

||*tʃiːpə *feəz|| ||*tʃiːp ə*feəz|| (cheaper fares, cheap affairs)

Words in company

3 If the unstressed syllable(s) is closely connected grammatically to the stressed word, although not a part of that word, they belong to the same rhythm unit:

||*gɪvɪt tə*dʒɒn|| ||*teɪkðəm fərə*wɔːk||
||*haʊ dɪdju:*mænɪdʒ təbɪ*ðeər ɪn*taɪm?||

4 Whenever you are in doubt as to which rhythm unit unstressed syllables belong to, put them after a stress rather than before it. So in *He was older than me*, if you are doubtful about ðən, put it with əʊldə and not with miː:

||hiːwəz*əʊldəðən *miː:||.

In many languages the rhythm unit is the syllable: each syllable has the same length as every other syllable and there are not the constant changes of syllable length which occur in English word groups. Some such languages are French, Spanish, Hindi, Yoruba. Speakers of these languages and others in which all the syllables have the same length will find English rhythm rather difficult, and they will need to work hard at it. If every syllable is made the same length in English it gives the effect of a machine-gun firing and makes the utterances very hard to understand. Some good work on English rhythm will help greatly in improving the sound of your speech.

Practise the following examples, beating the rhythm of the stressed syllables as you go and varying the lengths of the syllables so as to keep the stress groups equal in length:

	*teɪkɪt *həʊm		*teɪkɪt tə*dʒɒn		*teɪkɪt tə*dʒɒnsən	
	*laɪt ðə*faɪə		*laɪtɪŋ ðə*faɪə		hiːwəz*laɪtɪŋ ðə*faɪə	
	hiːwəz*məʊst ə*mjuːzɪŋ		hiːwəz*verɪ ə*mjuːzɪŋ	
	*dʒɒn wəz*leɪt		*dʒenɪ wəz*leɪt		*dʒenɪfə wəz*leɪt	
	hiːz*dʒʌst *ten		hiːz*dʒʌst *sevən		hiːz*dʒʌst *sevəntɪ	
	ɪtsə*haːd *dʒɒb				ɪtsə*trɪkɪ *dʒɒb		ɪtsə*dɪfəkl̩t *dʒɒb	
	ɪtwəzə*rɪəlɪ *gʊd *miːl		ɪtwəzə*rɪəlɪ *pleznt *miːl	
ɪtwəzə*rɪəlɪ *eksələnt *miːl	
	hiː*pleɪz *verɪ *wel		hiːz*pleɪɪŋ *verɪ *wel		hiːz*pleɪɪŋɪt *verɪ *wel	
	juː*dɪdɪt *raːðə *wel		juː*dɪdɪt *raːðə *betə				juː*dɪdɪt *raːðə *klevəlɪ	

6.6 Fluency

One other thing which you must pay attention to in saying word groups is that you say them *fluently*, *smoothly*, with no gaps or hesita-

Rhythm units

tions in the middle. When you know what words you have to say you should be capable of saying them without stumbling over the sounds and sequences of sounds. In English, as we have seen, one word is not separated from another by pausing or hesitating; the end of one word flows straight on to the beginning of the next. To improve your fluency try the method of lengthening word groups. Here is an example:

I went home – on the Sunday – morning – train.

First you say the short group *I went home* – smoothly; if you stumble, say it again, until you are sure that you can do it. Then add the next three words and say *I went home on the Sunday*, also without stumbling. Now add *morning* and say the whole thing from the beginning; and finally add *train*. Don't be satisfied until you can say it without hesitation and with your best English sounds and rhythm. Other examples for practice are on p. 106.

One difficulty which often affects foreign learners is connected with a vowel at the beginning of words, especially if it begins a stressed syllable. An example is: *He's always asking awkward questions* where *ɔːlwɪz, *ɑːskɪŋ and *ɔːkwəd all begin with a stressed vowel. English speakers glide smoothly from the final sound of the word before to the initial vowel of the following word with no break, no hesitation. Many speakers of other languages separate the two words by a glottal stop (see p. 14) and this gives a very jerky effect in English. You must try to go smoothly and continuously from one word to the other, with no glottal stop, no break.

 ‖hiːz *ɔːlwɪz *ɑːskɪŋ *ɔːkwəd *kwestʃənz‖

When the final sound of the word before is a consonant it will help if you imagine that it belongs to the following word, and we might transcribe our example: ‖hiː *zɔːlwɪ *zɑːskɪ *ŋɔːkwəd *kwestʃənz‖. This will stop you making a gap before the vowel.

If the final sound of the word before is a vowel there are various ways of avoiding the gap. In ðiː *ʌðə it may help to write a little /j/ before the /ʌ/: ðiː *ʲʌðə. The glide from /iː/ to /ʌ/ is very like a /j/ but a very gentle one. The same trick can be used after /ɪ/ and the diphthongs /eɪ, aɪ, ɔɪ/ which end in /ɪ/. ðeɪ *ʲɑː, maɪ *ʲɑːnt, ðə bɔɪ *ʲet ɪt (*they are, my aunt, the boy ate it*). However, we do distinguish between *my ears* and *my years*, etc., maɪ *ʲɪəz and maɪ *jɪəz, where jɪəz has a longer and stronger /j/ than the short and gentle glide before ɪəz.

Similarly, after /uː/ and the diphthongs /əʊ, aʊ/ which end in /ʊ/, we can use a little /w/-sound as the link, for example *two others*, *tuː

Words in company

*ʷʌðəz, *go in* *gəʊ *ʷɪn, *how odd* *haʊ *ʷɒd. Again we distinguish between *two-eyed* and *too wide:* *tuː ˑʷaɪd, *tuː *waɪd.

The vowels /ɜː/ and /ə/ can always be linked to a following vowel by /r/: *her own* həːr *əʊn, *for ever* fər *evə, and this is also true for /ɪə, eə, ʊə/: *clear air* *klɪər *eə, *share out* *ʃeər *aʊt, *poor Eve!* *pʊər *iːv. Again it may help to attach the /r/ to the following word: hɜː *ʳəʊn, *klɪə *ʳeə, etc. When /ɔː/ or /ɑː/ occur at the end of a word and a vowel immediately follows we also use /r/ as a link if the spelling has the letter r in it, but not otherwise, so /r/ occurs in *more and more* *mɔː ʳən *mɔː but not in *saw off* *sɔː *ɒf, and it also occurs in *far away* *fɑː ʳə*weɪ. When we go from /ɔː/ or /ɑː/ to a following vowel without a linking /r/ we glide smoothly from one to the other with no interruption of the voice by a glottal stop. Other examples for practice are on page 107.

6.7 Changing word shapes

We have already seen that some words have weak and strong forms depending on their place in the group and on stress. The shape of a word may also be altered by nearby sounds; normally we pronounce *one* as wʌn, but *one more* may be pronounced wʌm mɔː, where the shape of *one* has changed because of the following /m/ in *more*. Also *next is* usually pronounced nekst, but in *next month* may be neks mʌnθ, where the final /t/ has disappeared.

Alterations

Forms like wʌm mɔː where one phoneme replaces another mainly affect the alveolar sounds /t, d, n, s, z/ when they are final in the word: Before /p, b, m/

/p/ replaces /t/:	right place	raɪp pleɪs	
	white bird	waɪp bɜːd	
	not me	nɒp miː	
/b/ replaces /d/:	hard path	hɑːb pɑːθ	
	good boy	gʊb bɔɪ	
	good morning	gʊb mɔːnɪŋ	
/m/ replaces /n/:	gone past	gɒm pɑːst	
	gone back	gɒm bæk	
	ten men	tem men	

Before /k, g/

/k/ replaces /t/:	white coat	waɪk kəʊt
	that girl	ðæk gɜːl

Changing word shapes

/g/ replaces /d/: bad cold bæg kəʊld
 red gate reg geɪt
/ŋ/ replaces /n/: one cup wʌŋ kʌp
 main gate meɪŋ geɪt

Similarly, the sequences /nt/ and /nd/ may be replaced by /mp/ or /ŋk/ and /mb/ or /ŋg/ in *plant pot* plɑːmp pɒt, *stand back* stæmb bæk, *plant carrots* plɑːŋk kærəts, *stand guard* stæŋg gɑːd. Even the sequences /dn̩t/ and /tn̩d/ may be completely altered in a similar way in *couldn't come* kʊgŋk kʌm, *couldn't be* kʊbm̩p biː.

Before /ʃ, j/
/ʃ/ replaces /s/: nice shoes naɪʃ ʃuːz
 this year ðɪʃ jɪə
/ʒ/ replaces /z/: those shops ðəʊʒ ʃɒps
 where's yours weəʒ jɔːz

None of these alterations is necessary, so although you will hear English people use them, especially when they speak quickly, you need not imitate them.

In another kind of alteration the strong consonant of a pair replaces the weak consonant in compound words like *fivepence* faɪfpəns and *newspaper* njuːspeɪpə and in the closely connected *I have to, he has to*: aɪ hæf tuː, hiː hæs tuː. You should use these pronunciations, but do not make it a general rule to replace the weak consonant by the strong in other cases; you must distinguish between *the price ticket* and *the prize ticket*: ðə praɪs tɪkɪt, ðə praɪz tɪkɪt. Notice too that the English do *not* replace the strong consonant by the weak in phrases like *black box*, *great day*, which must be pronounced blæk bɒks, greɪt deɪ and *not* blæg bɒks, greɪd deɪ.

Some of the alterations mentioned here have taken place in the past inside English words, leaving them with a shape which is now normal. Examples are: *handkerchief* hæŋkətʃiːf, *special* speʃl̩, *soldier* səʊldʒə; you must use these forms, but there are others which you may hear which are not essential though you can use them if you wish. Examples are: *admirable* æbmərəbl̩, *Watkins* wɒkkɪnz, *broadcast* brɔːgkɑːst, *utmost* ʌpməʊst, *inmate* ɪmmeɪt.

Disappearances

The omission of sounds, as in neks deɪ, most often affect /t/ when it is final in a word after /s/ or /f/ (as in *last* or *left*) and the following word begins with a stop, nasal or friction sound.

Words in company

/st/ + stop:
    last time laːs taɪm   fast bus faːs bʌs
+ nasal:
    best man bes mæn   first night fɜːs naɪt
+ friction:
    West side wes saɪd   best friend bes frend

/ft/ + stop:
    lift boy lɪf bɔɪ   stuffed chicken stʌf tʃɪkɪn
+ nasal:
    soft mattress sɒf mætrəs   left knee lef niː
+ friction:
    left shoe lef ʃuː   soft snow sɒf snəʊ

The /t/ in /st, ft/ may also disappear when other consonants follow, but this is less common. Examples are: *last lap* laːs læp, *next week* neks wiːk, *best road* bes rəʊd, *left leg* lef leg, *soft rain* sɒf reɪn, *soft water* sɒf wɔːtə.

The /d/ in /nd/ or /md/ often disappears if the following word begins with a nasal or weak stop consonant:

/nd/ + nasal: blind man blaɪn mæn
    kind nurse kaɪn nɜːs
+ weak stop: tinned beans tɪn biːnz
    stand guard stæn gaːd
/md/ + nasal: skimmed milk skɪm mɪlk
    he seemed nice hiː siːm naɪs
+ weak stop: it seemed good ɪt siːm gʊd
    he climbed back hiː klaɪm bæk

The /d/ in /nd, md/ may also disappear when other consonants follow, but this is less common. Examples: *blind chance* blaɪn tʃaːns, *send seven* sen sevən, *hand-woven* hæn wəʊvən, *he blamed them* hiː bleɪm ðəm, *she seemed well* ʃiː siːm wel, *a framed picture* ə freɪm pɪktʃə.

When /t/ or /d/ occur between two other stop consonants they are never heard and you should leave them out, for example: *locked car* lɒk kaː, *strict parents* strɪk peərənts, *he stopped behind* hiː stɒp bɪhaɪnd, *dragged back* dræg bæk, *rubbed down* rʌb daʊn. It is not *necessary* for you to use any of the other reduced forms mentioned above, but if you find it easier to do so you may use the more common ones.

Similar disappearances have taken place in the past inside English words, leaving them with a shape which is now normal. Examples are: *grandmother* grænmʌðə, *handsome* hænsəm, *castle* kaːsl̩, *postman* pəʊsmən, *draughtsman* draːfsmən. In all these cases you should use this normal form. There are other cases where two forms may be heard: *often* ɒfn̩, ɒftən; *kindness* kaɪnnɪs, kaɪndnɪs; *asked* ɑːst, ɑːskt; *clothes* kləʊz, kləʊðz; and you can use whichever you find easiest.

Vowels have often disappeared from English words in the past, leaving a form which is the normal one, for example: *family* fæmlɪ, *garden* gɑːdn̩, *Edinburgh* edn̩brə, *awful* ɔːfl̩, *evil* iːvl̩, *interest* ɪntrəst, *history* hɪstrɪ. You should naturally use these normal forms. In other cases there are two possibilities, for example: *generous* dʒenrəs, dʒenərəs; *pattern* pætən, pætn̩; *deliberate* dɪlɪbrət, dɪlɪbərət; *probably* prɒblɪ, prɒbəblɪ; *properly* prɒplɪ, prɒpəlɪ. In these and similar cases it is best for you to use the longer form.

All these examples of changes and disappearances of sounds should encourage you to listen most carefully to the *real* shapes of English words, which are so often different from the shapes which the ordinary spelling might suggest. You can always find the normal shape of a word by looking for it in a pronouncing dictionary, for instance Daniel Jones's *English Pronouncing Dictionary*, which is most useful for any foreign user of English, but the most important thing, as always, is to use your ears and really *listen* to English as it is.

6.8 Exercises

(Answers, where appropriate, on p. 135)

1 Divide the following passage into word groups (p. 90).
   I have needed some new bookshelves for a long time. So during my holiday I decided to tackle the job myself. Not that I am very clever with my hands but it did not seem too difficult and as I had already said that we could not afford to go away I thought it would be prudent not to spend money having it done professionally. I bought the wood at the local handicraft shop and I had plenty of screws, but I found that my old saw, which had been left behind by the previous owner of the house, was not good enough and I decided to buy a new one. That was my first mistake, my second was to go to the biggest ironmonger in London and ask for a saw. You would think it was simple, wouldn't you, to buy a saw. But it is not. I said to the man behind the counter, 'I want a saw.' He was a nice man and did his best for me. 'Yes, sir, what kind of saw?' 'Oh, a saw for cutting wood.' 'Yes, sir, but we have fifteen different kinds for different jobs. What did you want it for?' I explained about my bookshelves and felt like an ignorant fool in a world of experts, which was true. He saw that I was a novice and was very kind. He

Words in company

told me what I should need and advised me to have a ladies' size. 'Easier to manage for the beginner, sir.' He was not being nasty just helpful and I was grateful to him. He also sold me a book on woodwork for schoolboys and I've been reading it with great interest. The next time I am on holiday I shall start on the shelves.

2 Each of the following examples contains one or more of the words which often have weak forms (p. 92). Transcribe the examples phonetically, showing the stressed syllables and the weak (or strong!) forms of those words:

They came to the door.
What are you surprised at?
She has an uncle and a cousin
Who will meet him at the airport?
What is her phone number?
I would like some tea.
What has John come for?
What can I do?
He was pleased, wasn't he?
When am I going to get it?
I have taken it from the shelf.
They had already read it.

There were two of them.
She is as old as the hills.
I shall be angry.
I will.
What does that matter?
Well, make some.
For his saw that you borrowed.
More than I can.
Of course he was.
I am not sure.
Yes, I thought you had.
But so had I.

3 Mark the words in the passage in Exercise 1 which should have a weak form.

4 Use the following lengthening word groups for practising fluency (p. 100):

I don't know – how – long – I need – to wait – for John – to come – home.

It was near the end – of the week – before – I arrived – back – from Scotland.

Who was that – awful woman – you talked to – all evening – at the party?

I can't understand – how you did it – so quickly – and efficiently, – Mr Southwood.

When did you hear – that story – about John – and the girl – next door?

Come and have dinner – with us – on Thursday – the twenty-third – of this month.

5 Use the following for practise in smoothness with initial vowels (p. 101):

Exercises

I was better off on my own.
Don't argue with anyone as old as I am.
How awful it is to be ill when everyone else is all right.
The hungrier I am, the more I eat.
Is there any flaw in my argument, Oscar?
Have you ever asked Ann about Arthur and Amy?
I owe everything I am to my uncle and aunt.
Come over to our house for an evening.
I haven't set eyes on Alec for ages and ages.
I ended up owing eighty-eight pounds.
You always ought to earn an honest living.

6 Arrange each word group in the passage in Exercise 1 into one or more rhythm units showing the stressed syllable and the unstressed syllables attached to it.
7 Which words in the passage might show *alterations* or *disappearances* in sounds (pp. 102 and 103)?
8 Transcribe the whole passage phonetically showing word groups, stressed syllables, rhythm groups and weak forms of words; then compare it with the version on p. 135 and notice any differences. Practise each word group aloud, concentrating on smoothness and rhythm.

7 Intonation

Every language has melody in it; no language is spoken on the same musical note all the time. The voice goes up and down and the different notes of the voice combine to make tunes. In some languages the tune mainly belongs to the *word*, being part of its shape, and if the tune of the word is wrong its shape is spoiled. The Chinese languages are like this and so are many others in south-east Asia, Africa and America. In these languages the same sounds said with different tunes may make quite different words: in Mandarin Chinese ma: said with a level tune means *mother* but ma: with a rising tune means *horse*, an important difference! In many other languages, of which English is one, the tune belongs not to the word but to the word group. If you say the English word *No* with different tunes it is still the same word, but nevertheless tune plays an important part in English. We can say a word group definitely or we can say it hesitantly, we can say it angrily or kindly, we can say it with interest or without interest, and these differences are largely made by the tunes we use: the words do not change their meaning but the tune we use adds something to the words, and what it adds is the speaker's feelings at that moment; this way of using tunes is called *intonation*.

English intonation is *English:* it is not the same as the intonation of any other language. Some people imagine that intonation is the same for all languages, but this is not true. You must learn the *shapes* of the English tunes, and these may be quite different from the normal tunes of your own language; and you must learn the *meanings* of the English tunes too, because they are important. For example, *thank you* may be said in two ways: in the first the voice starts high and ends low, and this shows real gratitude; in the second the voice starts low and ends high, and this shows a rather casual acknowledgement of something not very important. A bus conductor will say *thank you* in this second way when he collects your money and this is quite reasonable since he does not feel great gratitude. But if an English friend invites you to spend a week-end at his home and you reply with the second *thank you* instead of the first your friend will be offended because you don't sound really

Tune shapes

grateful. You may have made an honest mistake but it is difficult for him to realize that; he will think that you are being impolite.

7.1 Tune shapes

The shape of a tune is decided partly by the number of important words in the group and partly by the exact attitude you wish to express. What do we mean by 'important words'? These are the words which carry most of the meaning in a word group: for example, suppose that in answer to the question *How was John?* you say: *He was in an appallingly bad temper.* The first four words are not specially helpful to the meaning, not important, but the last three words *are* important; each of them adds quite a lot to the picture you are giving of John. Let's see how it might be said.

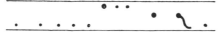

He was in an ap*pallingly *bad *temper.

This diagram shows the approximate height of the voice on each syllable: the first five syllables have low pitch; then there is a jump to the stressed syllable of *appallingly* and the next two syllables are on the same rather high pitch; then *bad* is a little lower and *temper* glides downwards from the stressed to the unstressed syllable.

Notice that there are three changes of pitch connected with stressed syllables. This shows that these words are important. An important word *always* has a stressed syllable and usually has a change of pitch connected to it.

Now suppose that the question is *Was John in a good temper?* In this case *temper* occurs in the question so that in the answer it is not specially important, it doesn't add anything to the picture, it gives little information; and the tune shows this:

He was in an ap*pallingly *bad *temper

Now there are only *two* changes of pitch, connected with the stressed syllables of *appallingly* and *bad*. So these two words are still marked as important, but *temper* is not. Although it still has the first syllable stressed, the fact that there is no change of pitch shows that the speaker is not treating it as important.

Lastly, suppose that the question is *Was John in a bad temper? Bad* and *temper* are not important in the answer because both are already in the questioner's mind, so the speaker says:

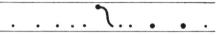

He was in an ap*pallingly *bad *temper.

Both *bad* and *temper* are still stressed, but they are shown to be unimportant because they have no change of pitch. Important words are not the same as stressed words. Stressed words may not be important, though important words *must* be stressed. It is not only the normally stressed words, like *appallingly* and *bad* and *temper* in our example, which may be felt to be important by the speaker; *any* word may be important if the situation makes it important. For example, if the first speaker refuses to believe in John's bad temper and says *He can't have been in an appallingly bad temper*, then our example would be:

He *was in an ap*pallingly *bad *temper.

Here the word *was* which is not usually stressed at all has both the stress and change of pitch which mark it as important, indeed as the only really important word in the group; and remember that when it is stressed it has its strong form.

In answer to the question *What is John like?* we might reply: *He seems very nice* and the usual way of saying this is:

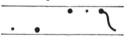

He *seems *very *nice.

Here *seems* is not marked as important; even though it is stressed it is on a low pitch like the unimportant initial words in our first example; the meaning of the group is approximately the same as *He's very nice*. But if it is:

He *seems *very *nice.

there is much more weight on *seems* because of the jump in pitch, and we understand that the speaker considers it important: he does so in order to emphasize that he is talking about the *seeming*, the *appearance*, and is not saying that John really *is* very nice. So the important words in a group affect the shape of a tune.

Now look at the following:

Tune shapes

*What's *that?   *What's *that?

In both these examples the words *what* and *that* are marked as important; *what* is stressed and on a high pitch and *that* has a fall in pitch in the first case and a rise in the second. So it is not only the *number* of important words which affects the tune-shape. The difference here is a difference of attitude in the speaker; the first example is a rather serious, business-like question, the second shows rather more interest and friendliness. So the attitude of the speaker, his feelings as he says the group, affects the tune-shape, and affects it very much, as we shall see.

Before we think about the speaker's attitudes let's see what tunes you must learn to use in speaking English: I cannot teach you *all* the tunes that English speakers use, but I shall describe the ones you *must* know to make your English sound like English.

7.2 The falling tune – the Glide-Down

In the shortest word-groups, where we use just one important word, the falling tune consists of a fall in the voice from a fairly high pitch to a very low one. The fall is on the stressed syllable or from the stressed syllable to a following one:

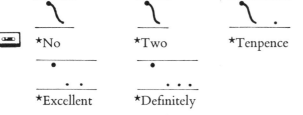

*No   *Two   *Tenpence

*Excellent   *Definitely

NOTICE
1 On a single syllable the voice falls within the syllable.
2 On more than one syllable the voice either falls within the stressed syllable or it jumps down from that syllable to the next.
3 Unstressed syllables at the end are all very low.

Start with *Tenpence and start by *singing* it – it doesn't matter if your singing is not very good, it will be good enough for this! Sing the first syllable on a fairly high note, but not *very* high. I cannot tell you exactly what note to sing because I don't know whether you have a

Intonation

naturally high voice or a naturally low one, but sing a note rather above the middle of your voice. Then sing the second syllable on the lowest possible note – growl it! Do this several times and hear the fall in pitch, then gradually go more quickly and stop singing. Say it, but with the same tune as before. Do the same with *Excellent* and *Definitely* and be sure that the unstressed syllables are as low as possible. Don't let them rise at the end; keep growling!

If there are other words following the fall they may still have stress, as in our previous example:

He was in an ap*pallingly *bad *temper.

But they are still said on that very low pitch, just like the unstressed syllables. Keep them right down.

Now try *No. Sing it on two notes, the high one, then the low one, as if it had two syllables, and again increase your speed and stop singing, but keep the same tune. Be sure that you finish with the pitch as low as you possibly can, right down in your boots!

When there is more than one important word in the group, the last one has the fall but the others are treated differently:

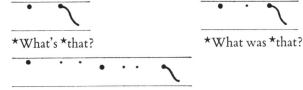

*What's *that?   *What was *that?

*What was the *matter with *that?

NOTICE
1 The stressed syllable of the first important word is high and any unstressed syllables following it are on the same pitch.
2 The stressed syllable of the second important word is a little lower and any unstressed syllables following it are on the same pitch.
3 The fall starts at the same pitch as the syllable just before it.

In groups with more than three important words the stressed syllable of each one is lower than the one before; this is why we call the tune the Glide-Down:

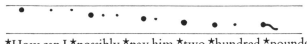

*How can I *possibly *pay him *two *hundred *pounds?

The Glide-Down

Start with **What's* said on a rather high pitch in your voice; keep the voice level, don't let it rise or fall. Then add **that* with the same fall as before. Then put *was* between the two, at the same level as **What* and the beginning of **that;* don't let it be higher or lower than **What*. If necessary start by singing it. Then try **What was the *matter with *that* in three parts: **What was the* all on the high note, then **matter with* all a little lower; put them together: **What was the *matter with* to form a high step followed by a lower step. Then add **that*, falling as before from the same pitch as *with*. Similarly practise the longest example in parts, each part a little lower than the one before, and the fall at the end from the pitch of the syllable before. Try to keep the unstressed syllables on the same pitch as the stressed ones, and not to let them jump either up or down. This treatment of the important words in downward 'steps' occurs also in other tunes, as we shall see later.

If there are any unstressed syllables before the stressed syllable of the first important word, these are all said on a rather low pitch:

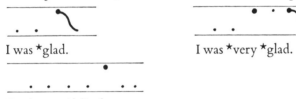

I was **glad.   I was **very **glad.

But it was ri**diculous.

Also, any stressed syllable near the beginning which belongs to a word which is not important is said on this same rather low pitch:

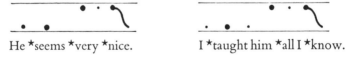

He **seems **very **nice.   I **taught him **all I **know.

NOTICE

These low syllables at the beginning are not at the lowest possible pitch like the ones at the end, but they must be lower than the high pitch which follows.

Practise these examples and be sure that the voice jumps upwards from the low syllables at the beginning to the first high-pitched stress.

We have a way of showing the Glide-Down which is simpler and quicker than the dots and lines used up to now. Before the stressed syllable where the voice falls we put (`). So: ||`No|| ||`Two|| ||`Ten-pence|| ||`Excellent|| ||`Definitely||. Notice that no other mark is needed

Intonation

to show the very low unstressed syllables at the end – any unstressed syllables after a fall are *always* low.

Before the stressed syllable of each other important word we put ('). So: ||'What's ˋthat|| ||'What was ˋthat|| ||'What was the 'matter with ˋthat|| ||'How can I 'possibly 'pay him 'two 'hundred ˋpounds||. Each of these marks shows a step, beginning with a high one and gradually coming lower until the fall is reached.

Unstressed syllables at the beginning have no mark before them: ||I was ˋglad|| ||I was 'very ˋglad|| ||But it was riˋdiculous||. If there is a low-pitched stress near the beginning (as in He *seems *very *nice) it is marked by (ˌ); so: ||He ˌseems 'very ˋnice|| ||I ˌtaught him 'all I ˋknow||. And the same mark is used for stressed syllables which come after the fall. So: ||He was in an apˋpallingly ˌbad ˌtemper||.

So with these few marks we can show all the features of the Glide-Down. In the following examples, first write them out in the longer way with dots and lines, to make sure you understand what the simpler system means, then practise them carefully:

||ˋTake it|| ||ˋHave them|| ||ˋSplendid|| ||ˋNonsense|| ||ˋWonderful|| ||ˋJohn's ˌcoming|| ||ˋSusan's ˌknocking at the ˌdoor|| ||ˋTen|| ||ˋTwo|| ||ˋFive|| ||ˋEight|| ||ˋSix|| ||ˋHalf|| ||ˋThis|| ||ˋWhich|| ||'Fifty ˋpounds|| ||'Seventy ˋfive|| ||'One and a ˋhalf|| ||It was imˋpossible|| ||I could have ˋcried|| ||They were in a 'terrible ˋmess|| ||I'll 'see you on 'Thursday ˋnight|| ||It's 'just 'after 'midnight|| ||There were 'too 'many ˋpeople ˌthere|| ||'Why did you 'tell him he was ˋwrong?|| ||It ˌwasn't 'half as 'difficult as I ˋthought it ˌwould be|| ||You can ˌphone me at 'any 'time of the 'day or ˋnight|| ||I ˌwaited ˌalmost 'twenty-'five ˋminutes for the ˌwretched ˌman||.

7.3 The first rising tune – the Glide-Up

The Glide-Up is just like the Glide-Down except that it ends with a rise in the voice instead of a fall. Both important and unimportant words before the rise are treated exactly as in the Glide-Down. An example is *But is it true that you're changing your job?*

But *is it *true that you're *changing your *job?

The last important word is *job* and here the voice rises from a low pitch to one just above the middle of the voice. Apart from this the tune is the same as in the Glide-Down: the unstressed syllable at the

The Glide-Up

beginning is low, and there is a step at the stressed syllable of each important word.

Similarly, *Are you married?* would be:

*Are you *married?

Notice that the stressed syllable of the last important word is low and that the voice jumps up to the unstressed syllable. And notice too that in *Have you posted it to him?* we have:

*Have you *posted it to him?

where again the stressed syllable of the last important word is low and each following unstressed syllable is a little higher, the last one of all being on the same fairly high note as in the previous examples.

Once again there may be stressed words within the rise, but they are not felt to be important:

*Have you been at *work to*day, *John?

Work is the last important word, and although *today* and *John* are stressed they behave just like the unstressed syllables of the last example and are not considered important by the speaker.

Practise with the following:

*Forty   *Forty of them

*Forty of them were *there

The first syllable must be low, and the last syllable fairly high; concentrate on these and let any syllables between these points take care of themselves. How you get from the low to the higher note at the end doesn't matter, but be sure that you start low and end fairly high (not *very* high!).

Now try the rise on one syllable:

*Two   *Five   *Eight   *Six

Intonation

If necessary sing the two notes as if there were two syllables and then gradually speed up and stop singing. Notice that the rise is slower on a long syllable like *Two or *Five, quicker on *Eight where the diphthong is shortened, and quickest on *Six where the vowel is shortest.

Now try adding other important words before the rise; say them as you did in the Glide-Down:

Are there *two of them?   *Can you be *here by *five?

And get the voice down low for the beginning of the rise.

In the simpler intonation marking, we use (‚) before the stressed syllable of the last important word to show where the rise starts and (·) before any stressed syllable within the rise. The other marks are the same as for the Glide-Down. So the examples used in this section are marked as follows:

||But 'is it 'true that you're 'changing your ‚job?|| ||'Are you ‚married?|| ||'Have you ‚posted it to him?|| ||'Have you 'been at ‚work to·day, ·John?|| ||‚Forty|| ||‚Forty of them|| ||‚Forty of them were ·there|| ||‚Two|| ||‚Five|| ||‚Eight|| ||‚Six|| ||'Are there ‚two of them?|| ||'Can you be 'here by ‚five?||.

Compare these with the fuller marking on the previous pages, then write out the fuller marking for the examples below and finally practise them carefully:

||'Who's ‚that?|| ||'Don't be ‚long|| ||'Give it to ‚me|| ||I'm 'just ‚coming|| ||Is 'anything the ‚matter?|| ||Can 'anyone 'tell me the ‚time?|| ||I was 'only 'trying to ‚help|| ||You can 'see it a'gain to‚morrow|| ||He's 'perfectly 'capable of 'looking 'after him‚self|| ||I ‚told him I was 'very 'pleased to ‚see him|| ||I 'shan't be 'any 'later than I ‚usually ·am|| ||'Did you 'say it was your ‚twentieth ·birthday to·day?|| ||'Could I 'borrow 'this ‚book for a ·day or ·two?|| ||'Would you 'mind if I 'brought my ‚mother-in-·law to ·see you?||.

7.4 The second rising tune – the Take-Off

After the Glide-Down and the Glide-Up we have the Take-Off; this also ends with a rise in the voice, like the Glide-Up, but any words and syllables before the rise are low. An example is:

The Take-Off

. . • . • . . ⌒

I was *only *trying to *help.

We call it the Take-Off because, like an aeroplane taking off, it starts by running along at a low level and finally rises into the air.

The rise, as in the Glide-Up, either takes place on one syllable, like *help*, or it is spread over several syllables:

. . ○ . ● . . ● . ˙ .

I was *only *trying to *help him with it.

Before the rise any stressed word is felt to be important, even though there is no change of pitch. All the syllables before the rise are said on the same low pitch as the beginning of the rise; they must not be higher than this, or you will have a Glide-Up instead of a Take-Off.

Practise the following and concentrate on keeping the syllables up to and including the beginning of the rise on the same low pitch:

. ⌒   . . . ●

It *was.   I was *trying.

. ● . ● . ˙ .

You *didn't *really *hurt your*self.

In the simpler intonation marking the rise has the same mark as before (,), any stressed syllables *after* this have (·), and any stressed syllables *before* it have (,). So our examples are marked:

||I was ,only ,trying to ,help|| ||I was ,only ,trying to ,help him with it|| ||It ,was|| ||I was ,trying|| ||You ,didn't ,really ,hurt your·self||.

Practise the following examples and be sure to keep the syllables before the rise low:

||You ,liked it|| ||You en,joyed it|| ||You were en,joying it|| ||I ,didn't ,hurt you|| ||,No-one's ,stopping you|| ||It was ,perfectly ,under,standable|| ||I ,wasn't ex,pecting him at ,six o,clock in the ,morning|| ||I ,didn't ,think he'd ,mind me ,borrowing it for a ,while|| ||You ,shouldn't have ,given him ,all that ,money, you ·silly ·boy||.

7.5 The falling-rising tune – the Dive

The last of our tunes that you must learn is the Dive. In its shortest

Intonation

form this consists of a fall from rather high to low and then a rise to about the middle of the voice.

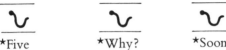

*Five   *Why?   *Soon

This fall-rise is connected with the stressed syllable of the last important word, like the fall and the rise of the other tunes. But it is only completed on one syllable if that syllable is final in the group. If there is one or several syllables following, the fall and the rise are separated:

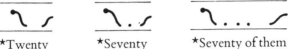

*Twenty   *Seventy   *Seventy of them

The fall is on the stressed syllable of the last important word and the rise on the last syllable of all. In the following examples:

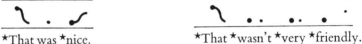

*That was *nice.   *That *wasn't *very *friendly.

there are stressed (but not important) words following the fall; in that case the rise at the end is from the last of the stressed syllables.

Words or syllables before the fall are said in the same way as for the Glide-Down and Glide-Up. Examples:

She was *quite *kind.

I *may be *able to *come on *Monday.

Notice that the fall of the fall-rise is always from a fairly high note.

If the stressed syllable of the last important word is final in the group, or if it is followed only by unstressed syllables, we put (ˇ) before it in the simpler intonation marking, so:

||ˇFive|| ||ˇWhy?|| ||ˇSoon|| ||ˇTwenty||
||ˇSeventy|| ||ˇSeventy of them||

But if the fall is followed by one or more stressed syllables we mark the fall with (ˋ) and we put (ˌ) before the last stressed syllable of all; any other stressed syllables have (ˌ) before them. So:

The Dive

||ˈThat was ˌnice|| ||ˈThat ˌwasn't ˌvery ˌfriendly||

Other intonation marks are the same as for the Glide-Down and Glide-Up:

||She was 'quite ˅kind||
||I 'may be 'able to 'come on ˅Monday||

Also:

||She ˌsaid she was 'quite ˈpleased aˌbout it||

Start practising on three syllables: fall on the first, keep the second low and rise on the third. Do it slowly and sing them if necessary:

	ˈShe ˌwon't ˌhelp				ˈI ˌdon't ˌknow	
	ˈThat's ˌno ˌgood				ˈThat was ˌnice	
	ˈJohn can ˌcome				ˈThis is ˌmine	

Notice that when the first syllable has a short vowel there may be a jump down to the next syllable rather than a fall. Compare:

ˈShe ˌwon't ˌhelp.   ˈThat's ˌno ˌgood.

When you are sure that you have the fall followed by the rise, speed up gradually to normal speed. Then try examples with two syllables, falling on the first (or jumping down from it) and rising on the second. Remember to start quite high:

	ˈYou ˌcan				˅Tuesday				˅Eighty	
	ˈI ˌcan't				˅Friday				˅Sixty	
	ˈJohn ˌdoes				˅Sunday	
	ˈThat's ˌnice				˅April	
	ˈPat ˌcame				˅August	

Next try the Dive on one syllable. Do it very slowly at first on three notes: high – low – high:

	˅Two				˅Four	
	˅Nine				˅Me	
	˅You				˅Soon	
	˅Please				˅Try	

Then gradually speed up and stop singing. Now try with short vowels:

Intonation

	ˇTen				ˇHim	
	ˇSing				ˇCome	
	ˇBad				ˇLong	
	ˇGood				ˇBob	
	ˇAnn	

The voicing of the final consonant will help you with those – the rising part of the Dive is on the final consonant, so use it.

More difficult are the short vowels followed by consonants with no voice, but you may lengthen the vowel a little to give you time to make both the fall and the rise:

	ˇSix				ˇWhich	
	ˇThis				ˇThat	
	ˇWhat				ˇUs	
	ˇStop				ˇYes	

Always be sure that you start high, go low and finish higher. Now some longer examples, which are easier, rather like a fall followed by a Take-Off. Keep the syllables after the fall down low until you reach the rise:

	ˇI ˌcouldn't ˌhelp it	
	ˇSomeone's ˌgot to ˌdo it	
	ˇMary would ˌprobably ˌtell you	
	ˇJohn ˌcame ˌhome to ˌday	
	ˇSeveral ˌpeople have ˌtold me they ˌthought it ˌlooked ˌpretty	

Now try adding other words before the fall-rise:

	'Don't ˇworry	
	'Don't be ˇlate	
	You 'mustn't ˇlose it	
	You can 'have it for a 'couple of ˇdays	
	'Try 'not to ˇbreak ˌthat	
	I 'went up to 'London by ˇcar to ˌday	
	'John 'told me he was 'going on ˇholiday ˌnext ˌweek	
	I 'hear there's 'been a 'great 'deal of ˇtrouble aˌbout ˌthat	

7.6 How to use the tunes

Statements

1 Use the Glide-Down for statements which are *complete* and *definite*:

How to use the tunes

‖It was 'quite ˋgood‖
‖I 'liked it 'very ˋmuch‖
‖I 'wouldn't 'mind 'seeing it aˋgain‖.

2 If the statement is intended to be *soothing* or *encouraging* use the Glide-Up:

‖I 'shan't be ˏlong‖
‖'John'll be 'here ˏsoon‖
‖I 'won't 'drive 'too ˏfast‖ (so don't worry).

3 If the statement is a *grumble*, use the Take-Off:

‖I ˏdidn't ˏhurt you‖ (so why make all that fuss?)
‖You ˏcan't ˏpossibly ˏdo ˏthat‖ (you ought to know better)
‖I ˏdid‖ (*grumbling contradiction*).

4 If the statement is *not complete* but leading to a following word-group, use the Dive:

‖I ˇlooked at him | (and recognized him at once)
‖She 'took the ˇcar | (and drove to London)
‖When'ever he 'comes to ˇvisit us | (he tries to borrow money).

5 If the statement is intended *as a question* use the Glide-Up:

‖You ˏlike it?‖
‖You 'can't ˏgo?‖
‖He 'doesn't 'want to ˏlend you it?‖

6 For statements which show *reservations* on the part of the speaker and which might be followed by *but . . .* or by *you must admit* or *I must admit* use the Dive:

‖He's ˇgenerous‖ (but I don't trust him)
‖He's ˇhandsome‖ (you must admit)
‖I could 'take you 'there toˇmorrow‖ (but not today)
‖I 'like your ˇhat‖ (I must admit)
‖It 'wasn't a 'very 'nice 'thing to ˇdo‖ (you must admit).

7 If the statement is a *correction* of what someone else has said, use the Dive:

(He's forty-five) ‖'Fortyˇsix‖
(I like him a lot) ‖You ˋused to ˏlike him‖
(I can't do it) ‖You 'can't do it ˋthat ˏway‖.

Intonation

8 If the statement is a *warning*, use the Dive:

||You'll be ˅late||
||I 'shan't 'tell you a˅gain||
||You 'mustn't ˅shake it ˌtoo ˌmuch||.

9 If the statement has two parts, of which the first is *more important* than the second, use the Dive, with the fall at the end of the first part and the rise at the end of the second:

||I 'went to ˅London on ˌMonday||
||You can ˅keep it if you ˌreally ˌwant it||
He was 'very ˅well when I ˌlast ˌsaw him||
||I'm 'very ˅comfortable ˌthank you||.

Wh-questions (containing Which, What, Who, etc.)

10 Use the Glide-Up if you want to show as much *interest* in the other person as in the subject:

	'How's your ˌdaughter?	
	'When are you 'coming to ˌsee us?	
	'When did you get 'back from ˌholiday?	

11 Use the Glide-Down if you want the question to sound more *business-like* and interested in the subject, and also for one-word questions (unless they are repetition-questions, see 12):

||'Why did you 'change your ˅mind?||
||'Who on 'earth was ˅that?||
||˅Which?||.

12 For repetition-questions, when you are repeating someone else's question or when you want the other person to repeat some information, use the Take-Off:

||ˌWhen did I ˙go?|| (Or where?)
||ˌWhy?|| (Because I wanted to)
(I arrived at ten o'clock) ||ˌWhen?||
(It took me two hours) ||ˌHow ˙long?||
(John told me to do it) ||ˌWho ˙told you to ˙do it?||.

Notice that in examples like the last three, where the other person is being asked to repeat information, the rise begins on the wh-word.

How to use the tunes

Yes-No questions (questions answerable by Yes or No)

13 For *short questions* used as responses, like *Did you?*, *Has she?*, etc., use the Glide-Down:

(John's on holiday) ||ˋIs he?||
(I went to the theatre last night) ||ˋDid you?||.

14 For all other Yes-No questions use the Glide-Up:

||'Have you ˏseen him ·yet?||
||'Did 'John 'post 'that ˏletter?||
||'Can I ˏsee it?||.

Notice that the Glide-Up is also used for repetition-questions of this type:
(Have you seen him yet?) ||'Have I ˏseen him ·yet?||
(Will you help me?) ||'Will I ˏhelp you?||.

Tag-questions (short Yes-No questions added on to statements or commands)

15 For tag-questions *after commands*, use the Take-Off:

||'Come over ˋhere | ˏwill you?||
||'Let's have some ˋmusic | ˏshall we?||
||'Hold ˋthis for me | ˏwould you?||.

16 If neither the statement nor the tag-question have the word *not* in them, use the Take-Off:

||You ˋliked it | ˏdid you?||
||They'd 'like some ˋmore | ˏwould they?||.

17 Where the word *not* occurs in either the statement or the tag-question use the Glide-Down to force the other person to *agree* with you:

||It's ˋcold toˏday | ˋisn't it?|| (*Forcing the answer Yes.*)
||It was a 'very 'good ˋfilm | ˋwasn't it?||
||You ˏwon't ˏworry | ˋwill you?|| (*Forcing the answer No.*)
||He 'can't 'really ˇhelp it | ˋcan he?||.

18 When you don't want the other person to agree with you, but to *give his opinion*, use the Take-Off:

||You're 'coming to ˋtea with us | ˏaren't you?||

Intonation

‖You 'weren't ˋhere on ˏWednesday | ˏwere you?‖
‖He ˌdidn't ˌlook ˌill | ˏdid he?‖.

Commands

19 If you want the command to sound *pleading*, more a request than an order, use the Dive, with the fall on *Do* or *Don't* if they occur, or on the main verb if not, and the rise at the end:

‖ˋShut the ˏwindow‖
‖ˋDo have some ˏmore ˏtea?‖
‖ˋSend it as ˏsoon as you ˏcan‖
‖ˋDon't ˏmake me ˏangry‖

Notice commands with only one important word:
‖ˇTry‖
‖ˇTake it‖
‖ˇLend it to them‖.

20 For *strong commands* use the Glide-Down:

‖'Don't be a 'stupid ˋidiot‖
‖'Take your 'feet off the ˋchair‖
‖'Come and have ˋdinner with us‖
‖'Have some ˋcheese‖.

Exclamations

21 For *strong exclamations* use the Glide-Down:

‖'Good ˋHeavens!‖
‖'How extraˋordinary!‖
‖What a 'very 'pretty ˋdress!‖
‖ˋNonsense!‖
‖ˋSplendid!‖.

Remember that *Thank you* comes in this class when it expresses real gratitude:
‖ˋThank you‖
‖'Thank you 'very ˋmuch‖.

22 For *greetings* and for *saying goodbye* use the Glide-Up:

‖'Good ˏmorning‖
‖'Hulˏlo‖

How to use the tunes

||'Good ˌbye||
||'Good ˌnight||.

23 If the exclamation is *questioning* use the Take-Off:

||ˌOh?||
||ˌReally?||
||ˌWell?||.

24 For exclamations which refer to something *not very exciting or unexpected*, use the Glide-Up:

	ˌThank you	
	ˌGood	
	'All ˌright	
	'Good ˌluck		.

The 24 rules given here for using the tunes will help you to choose a tune which is suitable for whatever you want to say. This does not mean that English speakers always follow these rules; if you listen carefully to their intonation (as you must!) you will notice that they often use tunes which are not recommended here for a statement or command, etc. You must try to find out *what* tunes they use and *when*, and just what they mean when they do it. But if you study the rules carefully and use the tunes accordingly you will at least be using them in an English way, even though you will not have the same variety or flexibility in their use that an English speaker has. This will only come with careful, regular listening and imitation. Don't be afraid to imitate what you hear, whether it is sounds or rhythm or intonation, even though it may sound funny to you at first. It won't sound half as funny to an English ear as it does to you, and in any case you'll soon get used to it!

7.7 Exercises

(Do not look at the answers on p. 136 until you have completed all these exercises.)

1 Practise again all the examples given in this chapter. Be sure that you understand the relation between the short and the long way of showing the intonation.
2 Transcribe the following conversation phonetically; divide it into word groups and rhythm units and then underline the important words:

Intonation

    Can you recommend somewhere for a holiday?
    What an odd coincidence! I was just going to tell you about our holiday!
    Really? Where did you go? The South of France again?
    No, this time we went to Ireland!
    Oh, you went to Ireland, did you? You were thinking about it the last time we met.
    Oh yes, I mentioned it to you, didn't I?
    You were thinking of Belfast, weren't you?
    Dublin. But we didn't go there in the end.
    Didn't you? Where did you go?
    Where? To Galway.
    That's on the West coast, isn't it? Was the weather good?
    Reasonably good.
    Tell me about the prices there, would you?
    They weren't too bad. You should go there and try it. But you ought to go soon. Summer's nearly over!
    It isn't over yet. But thank you very much for your advice.
    Good luck. Have a good time.
    Thank you. Goodbye.

3 Study the rules for using the tunes and then rearrange them so that all the rules concerning the Glide-Down are brought together; and similarly with those concerning the Glide-Up, the Take-Off and the Dive.

4 Using the rules, mark the intonation of each word group in the conversation in 2. After you have finished the whole conversation check your marking carefully with the answer on p. 136 and notice any differences. Then practise saying each part of it separately until you are satisfied that it is correct, and finally put the parts together so that you can say the whole thing fluently, rhythmically, and with English sounds and intonation.

Conversational passages for practice

Conversational passages

‖ˈðæts əˌnaɪs ˌsjuːt‖ aɪˈhævn̩t ˈsiːnɪt bɪˌfɔː| ˌhævaɪ‖
‖ˈnəʊ | ɪtsðəˈfɜːs ˈtaɪm aɪvˈwɔːnɪt ˌæktʃəlɪ‖ aɪˈəʊnlɪ ˈɡɒtɪt əˌbaʊt ˌfɔː ˌdeɪz əˌɡəʊ‖ juːˈlaɪkɪt | ˌduːjuː‖
‖ˈverɪ ˈmʌtʃ‖ ˈdɪdjuː ˈhævɪt ˈspeʃlɪ ˌmeɪd | ɔː ˈdɪdjuː ˈbaɪɪt ˈɒf ðəˈpeɡ‖
‖aɪˈhædɪt ˈmeɪd‖ aɪˈverɪ ˈreəlɪ ˌbaɪ əˌsjuːt | səʊaɪˈθɔːt aɪdˈhævɪt ˈteɪləd | ənaɪmˈkwaɪt ˈpliːzdwɪðɪt‖
‖aɪʃʊdˈθɪŋksəʊ‖ ɪtsˈverɪ ˈhænsəm‖ ˈmeɪaɪ ˈɑːsk ˈweə juːˌɡɒtɪt‖
‖ðəˈseɪm ˈpleɪs əzaɪˈɡɒt maɪˈlɑːstwʌn | ˈnaɪntiːn ˈjɪəz əˌɡəʊ‖
‖ˈnaɪntiːn ˌjɪəz‖ dəjuːˈrɪəlɪ ˈmiːn təˌtelmiː | juːˈhævn̩t ˈhæd əˈsjuːt ˈsɪns ˌðen‖
‖ˈðæts ˌraɪt‖ aɪˈdəʊnt ˈɒfn ˈweər əˌsjuːt juːˌsiː | səʊðeɪˈtend təˈlɑːst əˈlɒŋ ˈtaɪm‖
‖ˈnaɪntiːn ˈjɪəz ɪzˈsɜːtn̩lɪ əˈlɒŋ ˈtaɪm‖ ənˈiːvən ɪfjuːˈdəʊnt ˈweəðəm ˌmʌtʃ | jɔːrˈəʊldwʌn ˈmʌstəv ˈlɑːstɪd ˈwel‖
‖ˈəʊ | ɪt ˈdɪd‖ ðeɪˌdɪd əˈverɪ ˈɡʊd ˈdʒɒbɒnɪt‖
‖ˌwɒt wəzðəˈneɪm əvðəˈteɪlə‖
‖ˈfɪlɪpsn̩‖ɪtsˈkwaɪt əˈsmɔːl ˌʃɒp | ˈraɪt ətðiːˈend əvˈkɪŋ ˌstriːt‖
‖ˈaɪ ˌnəʊɪt‖ ˈrɑːðər əˈʃæbɪ ˌlʊkɪŋ ˌpleɪs‖ aɪvˈnevə biːnˈɪnðeə‖
‖aɪˈwʊdnt ˈkɔːlɪt ˈʃæbɪ | bətɪtˈɪzn̩t ˈverɪ ˈmɒdn̩ | aɪədˈmɪt‖ haʊˈevə | ðeɪəˈverɪ əˈblaɪdʒɪŋ | ənˌteɪk əˈɡreɪt ˈdiːl əvˈtrʌb‖
‖ˈsəʊ aɪkənˈsiː‖ aɪˈθɪŋk aɪlˈɡəʊ əˈlɒŋðeə‖ aɪˈniːd əˌnjuː ˌsjuːt‖ ˈəʊ | ˈbaɪ ðəˈweɪ‖ ˈwɒt ˈsɔːt əv ˈpraɪsɪz dəðeɪˌtʃɑːdʒ‖
‖ˈprɪtɪ ˈriːznəbl ˌrɪəlɪ‖ ˈðɪs wəzˈeɪtɪ ˈpaʊndz‖
‖ˈðæts ˌnɒt ˌbæd‖aɪˈθɪŋk aɪlˈlʊk ˈɪnðeə təˈmɒrəʊ‖
‖ˈjes | ˈduː‖ˈmenʃən ˈmaɪ ˈneɪm ɪfjuːˌlaɪk‖ ɪtˈwəʊnt ˈduːenɪ ˈhɑːm | ənɪtˈmaɪt ˈduː səm ˈɡʊd‖aɪvˈdʒʌs ˈpeɪd maɪˈbɪl‖

Conversational passages

 That's a nice suit. I haven't seen it before, have I?

No. It's the first time I've worn it, actually. I only got it about four days ago. You like it, do you?

Very much. Did you have it specially made, or did you buy it off the peg?

I had it made. I very rarely buy a suit, so I thought I'd have it tailored, and I'm quite pleased with it.

I should think so. It's very handsome. May I ask where you got it?

The same place as I got my last one, nineteen years ago.

Nineteen years? Do you really mean to tell me you haven't had a suit since then?

That's right. I don't often wear a suit, you see, so they tend to last a long time.

Nineteen years is certainly a long time; and even if you don't wear them much, your old one must have lasted well.

Oh, it did. They did a very good job on it.

What was the name of the tailor?

Philipson. It's quite a small shop right at the end of King Street.

I know it. Rather a shabby-looking place. I've never been in there.

I wouldn't call it shabby, but it isn't very modern, I admit. However, they're very obliging, and take a great deal of trouble.

So I can see. I think I'll go along there. I need a new suit. Oh, by the way, what sort of prices do they charge?

Pretty reasonable, really. This was eighty pounds.

That's not bad. I think I'll look in there tomorrow.

Yes, do. Mention my name if you like. It won't do any harm, and it might do some good. I've just paid my bill.

Conversational passages

‖aɪˈniːd əˈkʌpl̩ əvˋʃɜːts‖ˈgreɪ ˋterəliːn ˏpliːz‖

‖ˋsɜːtnlɪ ˏsɜː‖ aɪlˈdʒʌs ˈgetsʌm ˋaʊt‖ ˈwʊdjuː ˈmaɪnd ˈteɪkɪŋ əˏsiːt fərəˑmɪnɪt‖aɪˈʃɑːnt bɪˏlɒŋ

‖ˋnəʊ ˋdəʊnt bɪˏtuː ˏlɒŋ‖ aɪˈhævn̩t ˈverɪ ˈmʌtʃ ˋtaɪm‖

‖ˈverɪ ˏgʊd •sɜː‖ ˋhɪəz əˏnaɪs ˏʃɜːt‖wiːˈsel əˋlɒt əvˏðɪswʌn‖

‖ˋduːjuː ˏnaʊ‖ ˋjes ɪtsðəˈsɔːtəv ˋstaɪl aɪˏwɒnt bətaɪˈɑːst fəˋgreɪ‖ ˈðɪsɪz ˋpɜːpl̩‖

‖ˏpɜːpl •sɜː‖ ˋʃʊəlɪ ˏnɒt‖ ɪtsˈwɒt ˈwiːˈkɔːl ˈsɪlvə ˋbluː‖

‖welɪtˈlʊks ˋpɜːpl̩ təˏmiː‖ ˋenɪweɪ aɪdˈlaɪk ˈsʌmθɪŋ əˈlɪtl̩ ˈles ˋbraɪt‖ˈmɔː ˈlaɪk ðəˈwʌn aɪm ˋweərɪŋ‖

‖ˋəʊ ˋðæt ˏsɔːt əvˏgreɪ‖aɪˈhævn̩t ˈsiːn ˈðæt fəˋjɪəz‖

‖aɪˈbɔːtɪt ˋhɪə ˈsɪks ˋmʌnθs əˏgəʊ‖

‖ˈdɪdjuː ˏrɪəlɪ •sɜː‖ɪtˈmʌstəvbiːn ˈəʊld ˋstɒk‖

‖welˈsiː ɪfjuːˈvstɪl gɒtˈenɪ ˋleft ˏwɪljuː‖

‖ˋɑː ˏjes ˋhɪə wiːˏɑː‖aɪm ˋsɒrɪ əˏbaʊt ðəˏdʌst •sɜː‖ˈkænaɪ ˈlendjuː əˏhæŋkətʃiːf‖

‖ˈnəʊ ˏθæŋkjuː ˈaɪl səˏvaɪv‖ˋjes ˋðæt ˏlʊks ˏbetə‖ ˈhævjuː əˈnʌðəwʌn ˏlaɪkɪt‖

‖aɪməˈfreɪd ˋnɒt ˏsɜː‖ɪtsˈprɒbəblɪ ðəˋlɑːst ɪnðəˋkʌntrɪ‖

‖ˋəʊ ˈɔːl ˏraɪt‖ aɪl ˋteɪkɪt‖ˈhaʊmʌtʃ ˋɪzɪt‖

‖ˈtwelv ˋpaʊndz ˏsɜː‖ɪtwəzəˈverɪ ˈgʊd ˋʃɜːt ɪnɪtsˏtaɪm‖

‖aɪʃʊdˋθɪŋk ˏsəʊ ət ˏtwelv ˏpaʊndz‖ˈkænaɪ ˈpeɪ baɪˏtʃek‖

‖ˋsɜːtnlɪ ˏsɜː‖ juːˋhæv əˏtʃekkɑːd‖

‖ˋjes aɪˋhæv‖

‖ənˈwʊdjuː ˈdʒʌs ˈpʊtjɔː ˈneɪm ənəˈdres ɒnðəˏbæk‖

‖aɪkənˈnevər ʌndəˋstænd ˏðæt‖ˈɪf ðəˈtʃek wəzˈnəʊˇgʊd aɪdˈpʊt əˋfɒls ˏneɪm ənəˏdres ˈwʊdn̩t ˏjuː‖

‖jɔːˋdʒəʊkɪŋ ˏsɜːr əfˋkɔːs‖aɪnˈætʃərəlɪ əˈsjuːm jɔːˈtʃek ɪzˋgʊd‖

‖ˈverɪ ˋtrʌstɪŋ ˏɒvjuː‖ɪtˋɪz əzəˏmætər əv ˏfækt‖

‖ɪzðeərˈenɪθɪŋ ˋels juːˏniːd ˏsɜː‖ ˏtaɪz ˏsɒks ˏvests‖

‖aɪˏdəʊnt ˏθɪŋk •səʊ ˏθæŋkjuː‖ˈgʊd ˏmɔːnɪŋ‖

‖ˈgʊd ˏdeɪ ˏsɜː‖

I need a couple of shirts. Grey terylene, please.

Certainly, sir. I'll just get some out. Would you mind taking a seat for a minute. I shan't be long.

No, don't be too long. I haven't very much time.

Very good, sir. Here's a nice shirt; we sell a lot of this one.

Do you, now? Yes, it's the sort of style I want, but I asked for grey. This is purple.

Purple, sir? Surely not. It's what we call silver-blue.

Well, it looks purple to me. Anyway, I'd like something a little less bright, more like the one I'm wearing.

Oh, that sort of grey. I haven't seen that for years.

I bought it here, six months ago.

Did you really, sir? It must have been old stock.

Well, see if you've still got any left, will you?

Ah, yes, here we are. I'm sorry about the dust, sir. Can I lend you a handkerchief?

No, thank you, I'll survive. Yes, that looks better. Have you another one like it?

I'm afraid not, sir. It's probably the last in the country.

Oh, all right, I'll take it. How much is it?

Twelve pounds, sir. It was a very good shirt in its time.

I should think so, at twelve pounds. Can I pay by cheque?

Certainly, sir. You have a cheque card?

Yes, I have.

And would you just put your name and address on the back?

I can never understand that. If the cheque was no good, I'd put a false name and address, wouldn't you?

You're joking, sir, of course. I naturally assume your cheque is good.

Very trusting of you. It is, as a matter of fact.

Is there anything else you need, sir? Ties, socks, vests?

I don't think so, thank you. Good morning.

Good day, sir.

Conversational passages

‖ˈjɔːr ə ˌgɑːdnər| ˈɑːntjuː‖ dəˈjuːnəʊ ˈenɪθɪŋ əˈbaʊt ˈbɪzɪ ˌlɪzɪz‖
‖əˈbaʊt ˌwɒt | ˈbɪzɪ ˌlɪzɪz‖ wɒtɒnˈɜːθ ə ˈðeɪ‖
‖ˈəʊ | aɪˈθɔːtjuːd ˈnəʊ‖ ðeɪə ˈhaʊs ˌplɑːnts‖aɪvˈdʒʌsbiːn ˈgɪvn̩wʌn |
baɪmaɪ ˈsɪstər | ənaɪˈwɒnt təˈnəʊ ˈhaʊ təlʊk ˈɑːftərɪt‖
‖aɪməˈfreɪd aɪˈdəʊnt ˈnəʊ ˌmʌtʃ əˌbaʊt ˌhaʊs ˌplɑːnts‖bətaɪvˈgɒt
əˈbʊk ˌsʌmweə ðət ˌmaɪt ˌhelp‖ ˈlets ˈsiː‖ ˈɑː ˌjes | ˈhɪər ɪt ˌɪz‖
‖ðəˈkeər əv ˈhaʊs ˌplɑːnts‖ ˈmː | ˈðæt ˌlʊks ˌjuːsfl̩‖
‖dəjuːˈhæpən təˈnəʊ ðə ˌlætɪn ˈneɪməvɪt‖
‖aɪməˈfreɪd aɪˈdəʊnt‖ ˈbɪzɪ ˈlɪzɪz ðiːˌəʊnlɪ ˌneɪm aɪv ˌhɜːd‖
‖ˈwɒt dəzɪt ˈlʊk ˌlaɪk‖
‖welɪts ˌgɒt əˈrɑːðə ˈwɔːtərɪ ˈlʊkɪŋ ˇstem | ˈverɪ ˈpeɪl ˌgriːn‖ ənˈfeəlɪ
ˈsmɔːl ˈpɪŋk ˈflaʊəz‖
‖ˈhaʊ ˈmenɪ ˈpetl̩z‖
‖ˈgʊd ˈgreɪʃəs | aɪvˈnevə ˈkaʊntɪdðəm‖ˈfɔːr ɔː ˈfaɪv aɪsəˌpəʊz‖
ðeɪəˈrɑːðə ˈlaɪk ˈwaɪld ˈrəʊz ˌpetl̩z‖
‖aɪlˈlʊkʌp ˈbɪzɪ ˈlɪzɪ ɪnðiː ˈɪndeks‖ðeɪ ˈmeɪ ˌgɪvɪt‖ ˈjes | ˈhɪər
ɪt ˌɪz‖ˈpeɪdʒ ˈnaɪntɪ ˈeɪt‖ ˈðeər | ɪz ˌðætɪt‖
‖ˈmaɪ ˈwɜːd | ˈðæts əˌbɪgwʌn‖ˈmaɪnz ˈəʊnlɪ ˈgɒt ˈwʌn ˈstem | ənˈðæt
ˈsiːmz təˈhæv ˈdʌznz | bətaɪˈθɪŋk ɪtsðəˈseɪm ˇwʌn‖
‖welðeɪˈlaɪk ˇlaɪt | bətˈnɒt ˈhiːt‖ ˈwɔːtəðəm ˈwel ɪnðə ˇsʌmə | bətˈnɒt
ˈverɪ ˈmʌtʃ ɪn ˈwɪntə‖ ənˈðæts əˈbaʊt ˈɔːl‖ ˈəʊ | ˈðæts ˌrɑːðə ˌnaɪs‖
ɪtˈsez ˇhɪə | ðətðəˈdʒɜːmən ˌneɪmfərɪt | ˌmiːnz ɪnˈdʌstrɪəs ɪ ˈlɪzəbəθ‖
ˈmʌtʃ ˈgrændə ðənˈbɪzɪ ˇlɪzɪ‖
‖aɪˈθɪŋk aɪdˈrɑːðə hævəˈbɪzɪ ˇlɪzɪ ɪnmaɪ ˌhaʊs | ðənənɪnˈdʌstrɪəs
ɪ ˇlɪzəbəθ‖ bətˈθæŋkjuː ˈverɪ ˈmʌtʃ | aɪmˈverɪ ˈgreɪtfl̩ ˌtuːjuː‖ˈpræps
aɪlbiːˈeɪbl̩ təˈkiːpɪt əˈlaɪv ˌnaʊ‖ aɪˈjuːʒʊəlɪ ˈhæv ədɪ ˈzɑːstrəs ɪˌfekt
ɒn ˌplɑːnts‖
‖aɪʃʊdˈəʊnlɪ ˈwɔːtərɪt ˈwʌns əˈmʌnθ ˌnaʊ | ʌnˈtɪl ðə ˈsprɪŋ‖
ˈʌðə ˌwaɪz | juːlˈprɒbəblɪ ˈkɪlɪt‖
‖ˈgʊd | aɪlˈduː ˌðæt‖ ˈθæŋks əˈgen‖

You're a gardener, aren't you? Do you know anything about Busy Lizzies?

About what? Busy Lizzies? What on earth are they?

Oh, I thought you'd know. They're house-plants; I've just been given one, by my sister, and I want to know how to look after it.

I'm afraid I don't know much about house-plants, but I've got a book somewhere that might help. Let's see. Ah, yes, here it is. 'The Care of House-Plants'. Mm, that looks useful.

Do you happen to know the Latin name of it?

I'm afraid I don't. Busy Lizzie's the only name I've heard.

What does it look like?

Well, it's got a rather watery-looking stem, very pale green, and fairly small pink flowers.

How many petals?

Good gracious, I've never counted them. Four or five, I suppose. They're rather like wild rose petals.

I'll look up Busy Lizzy in the index. They may give it. Yes, here it is. Page ninety-eight. There, is that it?

My word, that's a big one! Mine's only got one stem, and that seems to have dozens. But I think it's the same one.

Well they like light, but not heat; water them well in the summer, but not very much in winter. And that's about all. Oh, that's rather nice; it says here that the German name for it means Industrious Elizabeth! Much grander than Busy Lizzie.

I think I'd rather have a Busy Lizzie in my house than an Industrious Elizabeth. But thank you very much, I'm very grateful to you. Perhaps I'll be able to keep it alive now. I usually have a disastrous effect on plants.

I should only water it once a month now, until the spring. Otherwise, you'll probably kill it.

Good. I'll do that. Thanks again.

Answers to exercises

Chapter 1 (p. 12)

1 *write*, 3 /r, aɪ, t/; *through*, 3 /θ, r, uː/; *measure*, 4 /m, e, ʒ, ə/; *six*, 4 /s, ɪ, k, s/; *half*, 3 /h, ɑː, f/; *where*, 2 /w, eə/; *one*, 3 /w, ʌ, n/; *first*, 4 /f, ɜː, s, t/; *voice*, 3 /v, ɔɪ, s/; *castle*, 4 /k, ɑː, s, l/; *scissors*, 5 /s, ɪ, z, ə, z/; *should*, 3 /ʃ, ʊ, d/; *judge*, 3 /dʒ, ʌ, dʒ/; *father*, 4 (f, ɑː, ð, ə/; *lamb*, 3 /l, æ, m/.

2 Some examples are: *for, four, fore* fɔː; *see, sea* siː; *sent, scent, cent* sent; *sole, soul* səʊl; *choose, chews* tʃuːz; *herd, heard* hɜːd; *meet, meat, mete* miːt; *too, to, two* tuː; *sight, site* saɪt.

3 raɪt, θruː, meʒə, sɪks, hɑːf, weə, wʌn, fɜːst, vɔɪs, kɑːsl, sɪzəz, ʃʊd, dʒʌdʒ, fɑːðə, læm.

mæt, met, miːt, meɪt, maɪt, kɒt, kʌt, kɔːt, lɪk, lʊk, bɜːd, bɔːd, ləʊd, laʊd, bɔɪz, bɑːz, beəz, ʃɪə, ʃʊə, kɒpə, griːn, tʃɑːdʒ, sɒŋ, faɪv, wɪð, truːθ, jeləʊ, pleʒə, hələʊ.

4 mʌðə, fɑːðə separate /m, ʌ, f, ɑː/.

Chapter 2 (p. 22)

2 Complete obstruction (glottal stop); vibration (voice); and open position (breath).

4 You cannot sing a voiceless sound; tune depends on variations in the frequency of vibrations of the vocal cords, and voiceless sounds have no vibrations.

5 It allows the breath stream to pass into the nasal cavity, or prevents it.

10 The tongue moves from a low to a high front position for /aɪ/, from a low back to a high front position for /ɔɪ/, and from a low to a high back position for /aʊ/.

12 The side teeth gently bite the sides of the tongue because the sides are touching the sides of the palate and the side teeth.

Answers to exercises

Chapter 3 (p. 63)

1 You should concentrate on the phoneme difficulties first.

Chapter 5 (p. 89)

4 bæg, bæk; kʌb, kʌp; hɑːv, hɑːf; lɒg, lɒk; kɔːd, kɔːt; pʊl, pʊʃ; luːz, luːs; sɜːdʒ, sɜːtʃ; seɪv, seɪf; raɪz, raɪs; dʒɔɪz, dʒɔɪs (*Joyce*); kəʊd, kəʊt; haʊz (vb.), haʊs (n.); fɪəz, fɪəs; skeəz, skeəs; bʊəz (*boors*), bʊəs (*Bourse*).

Chapter 6 (p. 105)

1, 6, 8 ‖aɪv*nl:dɪd səm*njuː *bʊk *ʃelvz | fərə*lɒŋ *taɪm‖ səʊ*djʊərɪŋ maɪ*hɒlədɪ | aɪdɪ*saɪdɪd tə*tæk! ðə*dʒɒb maɪ*self ‖*nɒt ðətaɪm*verɪ *klevə wɪðmaɪ*hændz | bətɪt*dɪdn̩t *siːm *tuː *dɪfɪk|t | ənəzaɪdɔː|*redɪ *sed ðətwiː*kʊdn̩t ə*fɔːd tə*gəʊ ə*weɪ | aɪ*θɔːt ɪtədbɪ*pruːdn̩t | *nɒt tə*spend *mʌnɪ | *hævɪŋɪt *dʌn prə*feʃənəlɪ‖ aɪ*bɔːt ðə*wʊd | ətðə*ləʊk! *hændɪ *krɑːft *ʃɒp ‖ənaɪhæd*plentɪ əv*skruːz‖ bətaɪ*faʊnd ðətmaɪ*əʊld *sɔː | wɪtʃədbiːn*left bɪ*haɪnd baɪðə*priːvɪəs *əʊnər əvðə*haʊs | *wɒznt *gʊd ɪ*nʌf‖ ənaɪdɪ*saɪdɪd tə*baɪ ə*njuːwʌn‖ *ðæt wəzmaɪ*fɜːst mɪ*steɪk‖ maɪ*sekənd | wəztə*gəʊ tə ðə*bɪgɪst *aɪən *mʌŋgər ɪn*lʌndən | ən*ɑːsk fərə*sɔː ‖juːd*θɪŋk ɪtwəz*sɪmpl̩ | *wʊdn̩t juː | tə*baɪ ə*sɔː | bətɪt*ɪznt‖ aɪ*sed tə ðə*mæn bɪ*haɪnd ðə*kaʊntə | aɪ*wɒnt ə*sɔː ‖hiːwəzə*naɪs *mæn | ən*dɪdɪz *best fə*miː‖ *jessɜː | *wɒt *kaɪnd əv*sɔː ‖*əʊ | ə*sɔː fə*kʌtɪŋ *wʊd‖ *jessɜː | bətwiːhæv*fɪf *tiːn *dɪfrənt *kaɪndz | fə*dɪfrənt *dʒɒbz‖ *wɒt dɪdjuː*wɒntɪt *fɔː‖ aɪɪk*spleɪnd ə*baʊt maɪ*bʊk *ʃelvz | ən*felt laɪkən*ɪgnərənt *fuːl | ɪnə*wɜːld əv*eksp3ːts‖ wɪtʃwəz*truː‖ hiː*sɔː ðətaɪwəzə*nɒvɪs | ənwəz*verɪ *kaɪnd‖ hiːtəʊldmi *wɒt aɪʃʊd*niːd | ənəd*vaɪzdmi tə*hæv ə*leɪdɪz *saɪz ‖*iːzɪə tə*mænɪdʒ fəðəbɪ*gɪnəsɜː ‖hiː*wɒznt *biːɪŋ *nɑːstɪ | *dʒʌst *helpfʊl | ənaɪwəz*greɪtfʊl *tuːɪm‖ hiː*ɔːlsəʊ *səʊldmi | ə*bʊk ɒn*wʊdwɜːk fə*skuːl *bɔɪz‖ ənaɪvbiːn*riː- dɪŋɪt wɪð*greɪt *ɪntrəst‖ ðə*nekst *taɪm aɪmɒn*hɒlədɪ | aɪʃl̩*meɪk ə*stɑːt ɒnðə*ʃelvz‖.

2 ‖ðeɪ *keɪm tə ðə *dɔː‖ ‖ðeə wə *tuː əv ðəm‖ ‖*wɒt ə juː sə*praɪzd æt‖ ‖ʃiːz əz *əʊld əz ðə *hɪlz‖ ‖ʃiː hæz ən *ʌŋk! ən ə *kʌzn̩‖ ‖aɪ ʃl̩ biː *æŋgrɪ‖ ‖*huːl *miːt ɪm ət ði: *eə *pɔːt‖

Answers to exercises

*aɪ *wɪl‖ ‖*wɒts ɜː *fəʊn *nʌmbə‖ ‖*wɒt dəz *ðæt *mætə‖
‖aɪ d *laɪk səm *tiː‖ ‖wel *meɪk *sʌm‖ ‖*wɒts *dʒɒn *kʌm fɔː‖
‖fər ɪz *sɔː ðət juː *bɒrəʊd‖ ‖*wɒt kən aɪ *duː‖ ‖*mɔː ðən *aɪ
*kæn‖ ‖hiː wəz *pliːzd *wɒznt iː‖ ‖əv *kɔːs iː *wɒz‖ ‖*wen əm
aɪ *gəʊɪŋ tə *get ɪt‖ ‖aɪm *nɒt *ʃʊə‖ ‖aɪv *teɪkən ɪt frəm ðə
*ʃelf‖ ‖*jes aɪ *θɔːt juː *hæd‖ ‖ðeɪd ɔːl*redɪ *red ɪt‖ ‖bət *səʊ
əd *aɪ‖

3 Have, some, for, a. To, the. That, am, but, not, and, as, had,
that, not, to, would, be, to. The, at, the, and, of, but, that, had,
the, of, the, not, and, to, a. Was, to, to, the, and, for, a.
Would, was, to, a. But, not. To, the, the, a. Was, a, and, his.
Of. A, for. But, for. And, an, a, of, was. That, was, a, and, was.
And, to, a. To, for, the. Not, and, was, him. A, for, and, have.
The, am, shall, a, the.

7 hæn(d)z, ɪtəbbɪ pruːdn̩t, spen(d) ðə mʌnɪ, dʌm prəfeʃənəlɪ,
hændɪkrɑːf(t)ʃɒp, aɪ hæb plentɪ, aɪ faʊn(d) ðət, əʊl(d) sɔː,
wɪtʃ əb biːn, lef(t) bɪhaɪn(d) baɪ, wɒzŋ̍k gʊd, fɜːs(t) mɪsteɪk,
wʊdn̩tʃuː, bɪhaɪn(d) ðə kaʊntə, bes(t) fə miː, wɒk kaɪnd,
dɪfrəŋk kaɪn(d)z, təʊl(d) miː, ədvaɪz(d) miː, wɒzmp biːɪŋ,
helpfl̩, greɪtfl̩, səʊl(d) miː, neks(t) taɪm.

Chapter 7 (p. 125)

2, 4 The number in brackets after each word group is the number of
the rule which has been used to select an appropriate tune.

‖ˈkænjuː rekəˈmend ˈsʌmweə fərə ˌhɒlədɪ (14)‖
‖wɒtənˈɒd kəʊˈɪnsɪdəns (21) aɪwəzˈdʒʌs ˈgəʊɪŋ təˈteljuː əˈbaʊt
ˈaʊə ˌhɒlədɪ (1)‖
‖ˌrɪəlɪ (23)‖ ˈweə dɪdjuːˌgəʊ (10)‖ ðəˈsaʊθ əv ˌfrɑːns əˈgen (5)‖
‖ˈnəʊ (1) | ˈðɪs ˌtaɪm (4) | wiːˈwent tuːˈaɪələnd (1)‖
‖ˈəʊ (21) | juːˈwent tuːˈaɪələnd (1) | ˌdɪdjuː (16)‖ juːwəˈθɪŋkɪŋ
ə ˌbaʊtɪt (4) | ðəˈlɑːs ˌtaɪm wiːˌmet (1)‖
‖ˈəʊ ˈjes (1) | aɪˈmenʃəndɪt ˌtuːjuː (1) | ˈdɪdn̩taɪ (17)‖
‖juːwəˈθɪŋkɪŋ əvbelˈfɑːst (1) | ˌwɜːntjuː (18)‖
‖ˈdʌblɪn (7)‖ bətwiːˈdɪdnt ˈgəʊðeər ɪnðiː ˌend (9)‖
‖ˈdɪdntjuː (13)‖ ˈweə ˈdɪdjuː ˌgəʊ (11)‖
‖ ˌweə (12)‖ təˈgɔːlweɪ (1)
‖ˈðæts ɒnðəˈwest ˈkəʊst (1) | ˌɪzn̩tɪt (18)‖ ˈwɒz ðə ˌweðə
ˈgʊd (14)‖
‖ˈriːznəblɪ ˌgʊd (6)‖
‖ˈtelmiː əˈbaʊt ðəˈpraɪsɪz ˌðeə (20) | ˌwʊdjuː (15)‖

Answers to exercises

||ðeɪˈwɜːnt ˈtuː ˌbæd (2)|| juːʃʊdˋgəʊ ˌðeə (1) | ənˋtraɪɪt (1)||
bətjuːˈɔːt təˈgəʊˇsuːn (8)|| ˈsʌməz ˈnɪəlɪ ˋəʊvə (1)||
	ɪtˌɪzn̩t ˌəʊvə ˌjet (3)		bətˈθæŋkjuː ˈverɪ ˈmʌtʃ fəjɔːrədˋvaɪs (21)	
	ˈgʊd ˌlʌk (24)		ˋhævə ˌgʊd ˌtaɪm (19)	
	ˋθæŋkjuː (21)		ˈgʊd ˌbaɪ (22)	

3 *Glide-Down:* Rules 1, 11, 13, 17, 20, 21.
Glide-Up: Rules 2, 5, 10, 14, 22, 24.
Take-Off: Rules 3, 12, 15, 16, 18, 23.
Dive: Rules 4, 6, 7, 8, 9, 19.

Appendix 1
The difficulties of English pronunciation for speakers of Arabic, Cantonese, French, German, Hindi and Spanish

On the following pages are very short summaries of the main difficulties in English pronunciation for speakers of six major languages (Arabic, Cantonese, French, German, Hindi and Spanish). Some of the consonants and vowels are referred to as equivalent in English and the other language, but you must understand that this does not mean that you need not bother with these sounds. It means that these sounds are independent in the language concerned, that they are a useful starting-point for acquiring the correct English sound and that they will probably not cause any misunderstanding if they are used in English.

In some cases an equivalent sound may be very different from the English one, e.g. the tongue-tip roll or tap for /r/ in Arabic and Spanish, but English listeners will nevertheless recognize it as /r/. Sometimes, also, the equivalent of the English sound is not the one which first comes to mind (or which is most often used by the learner), but it is there and can be found. An example is /ʌ/ for French speakers: they usually use a vowel which is quite foreign to English (the vowel in Fr. *œuf* 'egg') when the vowel in Fr. *patte* 'paw' would be very much nearer.

The main difficulties are listed and speakers of these languages are advised to pay special attention to those parts of this book which deal with these difficulties, but do not assume that these are the only difficulties; for everyone, including the many readers whose languages are not discussed here, the only reliable guide is a critical ear and, if possible, a good teacher.

Arabic (Cairo colloquial)

Consonants

EQUIVALENTS
/f, s, z, ʃ, h, t, k, b, d, g, tʃ, m, n, l, j, w, r/.

Arabic

DIFFICULTIES
1. /f/ and /v/ may be confused, /f/ being used for both, but /v/ may occur in Arabic in borrowed names.
2. /θ/ and /ð/ occur independently in some forms of Arabic (Iraqui, Saudi Arabian, Kuwaiti, etc.) but not in Egyptian Arabic, where they are replaced by /s/ and /z/.
3. /ʒ/ occurs in Arabic only in borrowed words and is often replaced by either /ʃ/ or /z/.
4. /p/ and /b/ are confused, /b/ being used for both.
5. /t/ and /d/ are dental stops in Arabic.
6. Stops are not generally exploded in final position in Arabic and the strong stops are often unaspirated.
7. /tʃ/ and /dʒ/ may be confused, /tʃ/ being used for both, though in practice /dʒ/ does not usually give difficulty.
8. /ŋ/ does not occur independently in Arabic and is replaced by /ŋk/ or /ŋg/.
9. /r/ is a tongue-tip roll or tap in Arabic and is often used before consonants and before a pause.
10. /l/ occurs in both its clear and dark forms in Arabic, but they are distributed differently and may sometimes be interchanged in English.

Sequences of three or more consonants do not occur in many forms of Arabic and careful attention must be paid to these, especially in order to prevent the occurrence of a vowel to break up the consonant sequence.

Vowels

EQUIVALENTS
/iː, e, æ, ɑː, ɔː, ʊ, uː, ə, aɪ, aʊ, ɔɪ/.

DIFFICULTIES
1. /ɪ/ and /e/ are confused, /e/ being used for both.
2. /æ/ and /ɑː/ are not entirely independent in Arabic and there is danger of replacing one by the other in some places.
3. /ʌ/ and /ɒ/ are confused, an intermediate vowel being used for both.
4. /ɑː/ is not always made long, and is then confused with /ʌ/ or /ɒ/.
5. /ɜː/ is replaced by a vowel of the /ʌ/ or /e/ type followed by Arabic /r/.
6. /eɪ/ is replaced by the usually non-diphthongal vowel in Arabic beːt 'house'.
7. /əʊ/ is replaced by the non-diphthongal vowel in Arabic moːz 'bananas', and this may cause confusion with English /ɔː/.

Appendix 1: Difficulties

8 /ɪə, eə, ʊə/ are replaced by the nearest vowel sound /iː, eɪ, uː/ + Arabic /r/.

Cantonese

Consonants

EQUIVALENTS
/f, s, h, p, t, k, b, d, g, tʃ, m, n, ŋ, j, w/.

DIFFICULTIES
1 No weak friction sounds (/v, ð, z, ʒ/) occur.
2 /v/ is replaced by /w/ in initial position and by /f/ in final position.
3 /θ/ and /ð/ are replaced either by /t/ and /d/ or by /f/.
4 /z, ʃ, ʒ/ are all replaced by /s/.
5 /b, d, g/ do not occur finally in Cantonese and are confused with /p, t, k/.
6 /p, t, k/ are not exploded in final position.
7 /tʃ/ and /dʒ/ are confused, /tʃ/ being used for both.
8 /l/, /n/ and /r/ are confused in some or all positions, /l/ (often nasalized) being used for all three. Before consonants and finally /l/ is replaced by /uː/.

The only consonants which occur finally in Cantonese are /p, t, k, m, n, ŋ/; the English final consonants and the differences among them need great care. Consonant sequences do not occur in Cantonese, and the English sequences, particularly the final ones, also require a great deal of practice.

Vowels

EQUIVALENTS
/iː, ʌ, ɑː, uː, ɜː, ə, eɪ, əʊ, aɪ, aʊ, ɔɪ, ɪə, eə, ʊə/.

DIFFICULTIES
1 /iː/ and /ɪ/ are confused; sometimes /iː/ is used for both and sometimes /ɪ/, depending on what follows.
2 /e/ and /æ/ are confused, an intermediate vowel being used for both; the same vowel also replaces /eɪ/ before consonants.
3 /ɒ/ and /ɔː/ are confused, an intermediate vowel being used for both.
4 /uː/ and /ʊ/ are confused; sometimes /uː/ is used for both and sometimes /ʊ/ depending on what follows.
5 /ɜː/ and /ə/ usually have lip-rounding. /ə/ is often replaced by other vowels because of the spelling.

Cantonese

6 The difference between long and short vowels and the variations of vowel length caused by the following consonant and by rhythm grouping are very difficult and need special care.

Cantonese is a tone language in which each syllable has a fixed pitch pattern. On the whole this does not make English intonation more difficult than it is for speakers of other languages, but it does affect the rhythm and particular attention should be paid to this.

French

Consonants

EQUIVALENTS

/f, v, s, z, ʃ, ʒ, p, t, k, b, d, g, l, m, n, j, w, r/. /tʃ/ and /dʒ/, although they have no equivalents in normal French words, do not cause difficulty.

DIFFICULTIES

1 /θ/ and /ð/ do not occur in French and are replaced by /s/ and /z/, or less commonly by /f/ and /v/.
2 /h/ does not occur in French and is omitted in English.
3 /p, t, k/ are generally not aspirated in French, which may lead to confusion with /b, d, g/ in English.
4 /t/ and /d/ are dental stops in French.
5 /ŋ/ does not occur in French and is replaced in English by the consonant at the end of French *gagne* 'earns'.
6 /l/ in French is always clear.
7 /r/ in French is usually a weak, voiced, uvular friction or glide sound.

Although sequences of four final consonants do not occur in French and sequences of three are rare, English consonant sequences cause little difficulty except when /θ, ð, h, ŋ/ are concerned.

Vowels

EQUIVALENTS

/iː, e, ʌ, ɑː, ɒ, uː, ə, aɪ, aʊ/. /ɔɪ/ has no obvious equivalent in French but causes no difficulty.

DIFFICULTIES

1 /iː/ and /ɪ/ are confused, /iː/ being used for both.
2 /æ/ and /ʌ/ are confused, /ʌ/ being used for both.
3 /ɒ/ is often pronounced in a way that makes it sound like English /ʌ/.

Appendix 1: Difficulties

4. /ɔː/ is replaced by the vowel + /r/ in French *forme* 'shape', when there is a letter *r* in the spelling, or by the vowel in French *beau* 'beautiful', when there is no *r*.
5. /əʊ/ is replaced by the non-diphthongal vowel in French *beau*, which causes confusion with /ɔː/.
6. /uː/ and /ʊ/ are confused, /uː/ being used for both.
7. /ɜː/ is replaced by the lip-rounded vowel + /r/ in French *heure* 'hour'.
8. /eɪ/ is replaced by the non-diphthongal vowel in French *gai* 'gay'.
9. /ɪə, eə, ʊə/ are replaced by the vowel + /r/ in French *lire* 'read', *terre* 'earth', *lourd* 'heavy'.
10. /ə/ is often replaced by other vowels because of the spelling.

Vowels are usually short in French, compared with English, and care must be taken to make the long vowels of English long enough.

Each syllable in French has approximately the same length and the same stress. English rhythm based on the stressed syllable and the resulting variations of syllable length cause great difficulty and must be given special attention, together with weak forms of words, which do not exist in French.

German

Consonants

EQUIVALENTS
/f, v, s, z, ʃ, ʒ, h, p, t, k, b, d, g, tʃ, dʒ, m, n, ŋ, l, j, r/.

DIFFICULTIES
1. /θ/ and /ð/ do not occur in German and are replaced by /s/ and /z/.
2. /b, d, g, dʒ, v, z, ʒ/ do not occur in final position in German, but the corresponding strong consonants /p, t, k, tʃ, f, s, ʃ/ do, which causes confusion between the two sets in English, the strong consonants being used for both.
3. /ʒ/ and /dʒ/ occur only in borrowed words in German and they may be replaced by /ʃ/ and /tʃ/.
4. The sequence /ŋg/ does not occur in German and is replaced in English by simple /ŋ/.
5. /l/ in German is always clear.
6. /w/ and /v/ are confused, /v/ being used for both.
7. /r/ in German is either a weak, voiced, uvular friction sound or a tongue-tip trill.

German

English consonant sequences cause no difficulty except when /θ, ð, w/ are concerned or when /b, d, g, dʒ, v, z, ʒ/ are part of a final sequence.

Vowels

EQUIVALENTS
/iː, ɪ, e, ʌ, ɑː, ɒ, ʊ, uː, ə, aɪ, aʊ, ɔɪ/.

DIFFICULTIES
1 /e/ and /æ/ are confused, /e/ being used for both.
2 /ɔː/ is replaced by the vowel + /r/ of German *Dorf* 'town' when there is a letter *r* in the spelling, or by the vowel of German *Sohn* 'son' when there is no *r*.
3 /əʊ/ is replaced by the non-diphthongal vowel of German *Sohn*, which causes confusion between /ɔː/ and /əʊ/.
4 /ɜː/ is replaced by the lip-rounded vowel + /r/ of German *Dörfer* 'towns'.
5 Non-final /ə/ is usually too like English /ɪ/, and final /ə/ usually too like English /ɒ/.
6 /eɪ/ is replaced by the non-diphthongal vowel in German *See* 'lake'.
7 /ɪə, eə, ʊə/ are replaced by the vowel + /r/ of German *vier* 'four', *Herr* 'gentleman', and *Uhr* 'clock'.

German has long and short vowels as in English, but the influence of following consonants is not so great and care must be taken in particular to shorten the long vowels when they are followed by strong consonants.

A stressed vowel at the beginning of a word and sometimes within a word is preceded by a glottal stop. This must be avoided in English for the sake of smoothness.

Hindi

Consonants

EQUIVALENTS
/s, z, ʃ, h, p, t, k, b, d, g, tʃ, dʒ, m, n, l, j, r/.

DIFFICULTIES
1 /f/ and /p/ are confused, /p/ being used for both.
2 /θ/ and /ð/ are replaced by dental stops, which causes confusion with /t/ and /d/.
3 /z/ is sometimes replaced by /dʒ/ or /dz/.

Appendix 1: Difficulties

4 /ʒ/ and /z/ are confused, /z/ (or sometimes /dʒ/ or /dz/) being used for both.
5 /t/ and /d/ are made with the extreme edge of the tongue-tip curled back to a point just behind the alveolar ridge. These *retroflex* sounds colour the whole speech and should be avoided.
6 /p, t, k/ are often made with no aspiration even though the aspirated consonants occur in Hindi; this may cause confusion with /b, d, g/.
7 /ŋ/ may occur in final position, but between vowels it is always replaced by /ŋg/.
8 /l/ is always clear in Hindi.
9 /w/ and /v/ are confused, an intermediate sound being used for both.
10 /r/ is often like the English sound in initial position, but elsewhere is a tongue-tip trill or tap.
11 Final consonants are often followed by /ə/ when they should not be, causing confusion between e.g. *bit* and *bitter*.

Vowels

EQUIVALENTS

/iː, ɪ, æ, ʌ, ɑː, ʊ, uː, ə, aɪ, aʊ/. /ɔɪ/ has no obvious equivalent in Hindi but causes no difficulty.

DIFFICULTIES

1 /e/ is replaced by either /æ/ or /eɪ/.
2 /ɑː, ɒ, ɔː/ are confused.
3 /ɜː/ is replaced by /ʌ/+Hindi /r/.
4 /ə/ in final position is often a shortened form of /ɑː/, and in all positions may be replaced by other vowels because of the spelling.
5 /eɪ/ is replaced by the non-diphthongal vowel in Hindi re̱l 'train', and as this vowel is often quite short it may be confused with English /e/.
6 /əʊ/ is replaced by the non-diphthongal vowel in Hindi lo̱g 'people'.
7 /ɪə, eə, ʊə/ are replaced by /iːʌr, eʌr, uːʌr/.

The English long vowels are made much too short by Hindi speakers, especially in final position, and care must be taken to lengthen them considerably whenever they are fully long in English.

Rhythm in Hindi is more like that of French than English. There is much less variation of length and stress and no grouping of syllables into rhythm units as in English. The wrong syllable of a word is often stressed and great care must be taken with this and with rhythm in general. There is also difficulty in identifying the important words on which tune shape partly depends.

Spanish

Consonants

EQUIVALENTS
/f, θ, s, h, p, t, k, g, tʃ, m, n, l, j, w, r/.

DIFFICULTIES
1. /v/ and /b/ are confused; sometimes /b/ replaces /v/ and sometimes the reverse. /b/ must be a complete stop in all positions, and /v/ a lip-teeth friction sound.
2. /ð/ and /d/ are confused; sometimes /d/ (a very dental variety) replaces /ð/ and sometimes the reverse. /d/ must be a complete alveolar stop in all positions, and /ð/ a dental friction sound.
3. /g/ is often replaced by a similar friction sound; this does not generally lead to misunderstanding but should be avoided; /g/ must be a complete stop in all positions.
4. /s/ and /z/ are confused, /s/ usually being used for both, though only /z/ occurs before voiced consonants. /s/ before other consonants is very weak and in Latin American Spanish is often replaced by /h/.
5. /ʒ/ occurs in Argentinian Spanish but not elsewhere and both /ʃ/ and /ʒ/ are then replaced by /s/.
6. /dʒ/ and /tʃ/ are confused, /tʃ/ being used for both.
7. In Latin American Spanish /h/ is usually acceptable for English. In Peninsular Spanish /h/ is replaced by a strong voiceless friction sound made between the back of the tongue and the soft palate. This does not cause confusion, but gives a disagreeable effect, and the mouth friction must be avoided.
8. /t/ is very dental in Spanish.
9. /ŋ/ does not occur independently in Spanish and is replaced by /n/ or /ŋg/.
10. /l/ is always clear in Spanish.
11. /r/ in Spanish is a tongue-tip roll or tap.
12. /p, t, k/ are not aspirated in Spanish.

Consonant sequences in Spanish consist of an initial stop or /f/+/r, l, w/ or /j/. Other initial consonants may be followed only by /j/ or /w/. Many of the English initial sequences and almost all final sequences are very difficult and need much practice.

Appendix 1: Difficulties

Vowels

EQUIVALENTS

/iː, e, ʌ, ɒ, uː, eɪ, aɪ, aʊ, ɔɪ/.

DIFFICULTIES

1. /iː/ and /ɪ/ are confused, the replacement being a vowel usually more like /iː/ than /ɪ/.
2. /æ/, /ʌ/ and /ɑː/ (if there is no letter *r* in the spelling) are all confused, /ʌ/ being used for all three. Where *r* occurs in the spelling, /ɑː/ is replaced by the vowel+/r/ of Spanish *carta* 'letter'.
3. /ɒ/, /əʊ/ and /ɔː/ (if there is no letter *r* in the spelling) are all confused, a vowel intermediate between /ɒ/ and /ɔː/ being used for all three. Where *r* occurs in the spelling /ɔː/ is replaced by the vowel+/r/ of Spanish *porque* 'because'.
4. /uː/ and /ʊ/ are confused, the replacement being a vowel usually more like /uː/ than /ʊ/.
5. /ɜː/ is replaced by the vowel + /r/ of Spanish *ser* 'be'.
6. /ə/ is usually replaced by some other vowel suggested by the spelling (with /r/ added if the spelling has *r*).
7. /ɪə, eə, ʊə/ are replaced by the vowel + /r/ of Spanish *ir* 'go', *ser* 'be', *duro* 'hard'.
8. There is no distinction between long and short vowels in Spanish, and all vowels have the same length as the English short vowels.

Special attention must be given to lengthening the long vowels. Rhythm in Spanish is like that of French or Hindi. Stressed syllables occur, but each syllable has approximately the same length and there is none of the variation in length which results in English from the grouping of syllables into rhythm units. Special attention must be given to this, to the use of /ə/ in weak syllables and to the weak forms of unstressed words, which do not occur in Spanish.

Appendix 2
Useful materials for further study

Textbooks

Gimson, A. C. *An Introduction to the Pronunciation of English.* Edward Arnold, 1970
Jones, D. *An Outline of English Phonetics.* Cambridge University Press, 9th edn, 1975
Jones, D. *English Pronouncing Dictionary.* Dent, 14th edn, 1977
Kenyon, J. S. *American Pronunciation.* Wahr, 10th edn, 1958
MacCarthy, P. A. D. *The Teaching of Pronunciation.* Cambridge University Press, 1978
O'Connor, J. D. and Arnold, G. F. *Intonation of Colloquial English.* Longman, 1973 (with recording)
Roach, P. *English Phonetics and Phonology.* Cambridge University Press, 1983

Practice books (with recordings)

Arnold, G. F. and Gimson, A. C. *English Pronunciation Practice.* University of London Press, 1973
Baker, A. *Introducing English Pronunciation.* Cambridge University Press, 1982
Baker, A. *Ship or Sheep?* Cambridge University Press, 2nd edn, 1981
Baker, A. *Tree or Three?* Cambridge University Press, 1981
Barnard, G. L. and McKay, P. S. *Practice in Spoken English.* Macmillan, 1963
Gimson, A. C. *A Practical Course of English Pronunciation.* Edward Arnold, 1975
Hill, L. A. *Drills and Tests in English Sounds.* Longman, 1967
Mortimer, C. *Elements of Pronunciation.* Cambridge University Press, 1985
Trim, J. L. M. *English Pronunciation Illustrated.* Cambridge University Press, 1975

Appendix 2: Useful materials

Phonetic readers (with intonation marking and recordings)

O'Connor, J. D. *Phonetic Drill Reader*. Cambridge University Press, 1973
O'Connor, J. D. *Advanced Phonetic Reader*. Cambridge University Press, 1971

Glossary

alveolar ridge: see *palate.*
aspiration: short period after the explosion of /p, t, k/ when air leaves the mouth without voice.
consonant: one of a set of sounds in which air from the lungs is seriously obstructed in the mouth, and which occur in similar positions in words.
diphthong: a smooth glide from one vowel position to another, the whole glide acting like one of the long, simple vowels.
Dive: the falling-rising tune in intonation.
friction consonants: sounds made by narrowing the air passage until the air is interfered with and causes friction.
Glide-Down: the falling tune in intonation.
Glide-Up: one of the two rising tunes.
gliding consonants: consonants with no stop or friction which have a rapid glide to a vowel.
glottal stop: air from the lungs is compressed below the closed vocal cords and then bursts out with an explosion.
glottis: the space between the vocal cords.
intonation: the patterns of pitch on word groups which give information about the speaker's feelings.
larynx: structure at the top of the wind-pipe from the lungs, which contains the vocal cords.
lateral consonant: a consonant (/l/) in which the tongue-tip blocks the centre of the mouth and air goes over the sides of the tongue.
lateral explosion: the release of /t/ or /d/, when followed by /l/, by lowering only the sides of the tongue, causing the compressed air to burst out over the sides.
nasal consonant: a consonant in which the mouth is blocked and all the air goes out through the nose.
nasal explosion: the release of a stop consonant by lowering the soft palate, causing the compressed air to burst out through the nose.
nasalized vowel: a vowel in which the soft palate is lowered and air goes out through both the mouth and the nose.

Glossary

palate: the roof of the mouth, divided into the soft palate at the back, the hard palate in the middle, and the alveolar ridge, just behind the teeth.

phoneme: a set of similar sounds which contrasts with other such sets to differentiate words.

phonemic transcription: the representation of each phoneme by a single symbol.

Received Pronunciation: that kind of pronunciation which is used by many educated speakers, particularly in south-east England. Sometimes called B.B.C. English.

rhythm unit: one stressed syllable which may have unstressed syllables before and/or after it.

stop consonants: consonants in which the air is completely blocked and therefore compressed and released with an explosion.

stress: greater effort on a syllable or syllables in a word or longer utterance than on the other syllables.

stress group: the stressed syllable and any syllable(s) which follow it in a rhythm unit.

strong consonant: a consonant in which air is pushed out by the lungs with considerable force.

strong form: see *weak form.*

syllabic consonant: normally a syllable contains a vowel; sometimes /n/ or /l/ replace the vowel – they are then syllabics (e.g. in rɪtn̩, mɪdl̩).

syllable: a unit consisting of one vowel or syllabic consonant which may be preceded and/or followed by a consonant or consonants.

Take-Off: the second rising tune in intonation.

tongue: when the tongue is at rest, the *back* is under the soft palate, the *front* under the hard palate, and the *blade* under the alveolar ridge. The *tip* is the part right at the front of the blade.

vocal cords: bands of elastic tissue in the larynx which can vibrate, causing voice, can allow free passage of the air, for voiceless sounds, and can completely stop the air-flow, giving the glottal stop.

voice: musical note generated by vibration of the vocal cords. Voiced sounds have this vibration (e.g. /m, l, ɑː/), voiceless sounds do not (e.g. /p, s, tʃ/).

vowel: one of a set of voiced sounds in which air leaves the mouth with no interference and which occur in similar positions in words.

weak consonants: consonants in which air is pushed out by the lungs with little force.

weak form: certain words are pronounced differently when they are not stressed. This unstressed pronunciation is the weak form, and the stressed pronunciation is the strong form.